Being Buddha at Work

Being Buddha at Work

108 *Ancient Truths on Change, Stress, Money, and Success*

Franz Metcalf and BJ Gallagher

BK

Berrett–Koehler Publishers, Inc.
San Francisco
a BK Life book

Berrett-Koehler Publishers, Inc.
235 Montgomery Street, Suite 650
San Francisco, CA 94104-2916
Tel: (415) 288-0260   Fax: (415) 362-2512   www.bkconnection.com

Ordering Information

Quantity sales. Special discounts are available on quantity purchases by corporations, associations, and others. For details, contact the "Special Sales Department" at the Berrett-Koehler address above.

Individual sales. Berrett-Koehler publications are available through most bookstores. They can also be ordered directly from Berrett-Koehler: Tel: (800) 929-2929; Fax: (802) 864-7626; www.bkconnection.com

Orders for college textbook/course adoption use. Please contact Berrett-Koehler: Tel: (800) 929-2929; Fax: (802) 864-7626.

Orders by U.S. trade bookstores and wholesalers. Please contact Ingram Publisher Services, Tel: (800) 509-4887; Fax: (800) 838-1149; E-mail: customer.service@ ingrampublisherservices.com; or visit www.ingrampublisherservices.com/Ordering for details about electronic ordering.

Berrett-Koehler and the BK logo are registered trademarks of Berrett-Koehler Publishers, Inc.

Printed in the United States of America

Berrett-Koehler books are printed on long-lasting acid-free paper. When it is available, we choose paper that has been manufactured by environmentally responsible processes. These may include using trees grown in sustainable forests, incorporating recycled paper, minimizing chlorine in bleaching, or recycling the energy produced at the paper mill.

Library of Congress Cataloging-in-Publication Data

Metcalf, Franz.
   Being Buddha at work : 108 ancient truths on change, stress, money, and success / Franz Metcalf and BJ Gallagher. — 1st ed.
      p. cm.
   Includes bibliographical references.
   ISBN 978-1-60994-292-2 (pbk.)
1. Work—Religious aspects—Buddhism. 2. Interpersonal relations—Religious aspects—Buddhism. 3. Leadership—Religious aspects—Buddhism. 4. Success—Religious aspects—Buddhism. 5. Organizational change. I. Gallagher, B. J. (Barbara J.), 1949– II. Title.
   BQ5400.M48 2011
   294.3'444—dc23   2011045762

FIRST EDITION

16 15 14 13 12   10 9 8 7 6 5 4 3 2 1

Cover design: Ian Shimkoviak/The Book Designer
Copyediting: Elissa Rabellino
Interior design and composition: Leigh McLellan Design

*We dedicate this book
to all workers throughout space and time,
to those who work to live
and those who live to work.*

*May the Buddha's words and wisdom
reach your eyes,
awaken your minds,
and guide your feet
along the path.*

Contents

PART I ❉ Becoming a Mindful Worker

PART II ✿ Cultivating Mindful Work Relationships

THE DALAI LAMA

Foreword

MORE THAN 2500 years have passed since the Buddha lived and taught in India. We Buddhists remember the Buddha as a great teacher who showed the path to ultimate peace and happiness for all sentient beings. His teaching remains refreshing and relevant even today because he invited people to listen, reflect, and critically examine what he had to say in the context of their own lives.

It is a fundamental truth that whatever our social status, background, age, or gender, we all want happiness and dislike suffering. However, all of us regularly experience suffering and are caught in the sway of disturbing emotions. Like all religions, Buddhism deals with basic human problems, but what distinguishes the Buddhist way of thinking is its employment of human intelligence in dealing with our disturbing emotions. In addition, the Buddhist view of interdependence and the advice not to harm anyone emphasize the practice of compassion and nonviolence. This remains one of the most potent forces for good in the world today.

From a Buddhist viewpoint, all that we do originates in the mind. The quality of our actions depends primarily on our motivation. If we develop a good heart, then, whatever field we work in, the result will be more beneficial. With proper motivation, our activities will be helpful; without it, we are likely to make trouble. This is why the idea of compassion is so important. Although it is difficult to bring about the inner change that gives rise to it, it is absolutely worthwhile to try.

The ultimate purpose of the Buddha's teachings is to serve and benefit humanity, which entails applying them in practice in our day-to-day lives. This in turn reflects a practical approach to human problems, and I don't believe you need to be a Buddhist to benefit from such an approach. This book, *Being Buddha at Work*, attempts to relate the Buddha's advice to the modern workplace. I trust that readers will find inspiration here and pray that those who do will meet with success in putting that inspiration into effect.

October 27, 2011

Putting Buddha to Work

THIS BOOK IS for people who seek to apply ancient spiritual wisdom to current workplace situations. Sometimes this means ancient solutions to today's problems. Sometimes it means new perspectives on timeless troubles. In all cases, we put Buddha to work because he was not some solitary hermit; he was the founder and CEO of a growing organization. As you get into this book, you'll see what we mean.

Most people who perform paid work outside the home spend more of their waking time at work than anywhere else. They see their bosses more than they do their spouses. They spend more time and energy dealing with difficult coworkers than they do with their own difficult children. For many of us, work itself has become an important way to establish personal identity, to meet social needs, to build satisfaction through accomplishment, and to find purpose and meaning in life. It's also a place where we face the fundamental truths of the world according to Buddhism: everything is frustrating, everything is interconnected, and everything is impermanent. (Note that these are translations of *dukkha*, *anatta*, and *anicca*, the "three marks" of existence. See the glossary for more information on these and many other Buddhist terms.)

It should come as no surprise, then, that workers at all levels, in all kinds of organizations, are bringing their spiritual beliefs and values to work, or are seeking to discover new beliefs and values *through* their work. Many people see work as a place where they can live out their personal spirituality or their relationship with ultimate reality (however they define it); some even see their place of work as their primary spiritual community. We agree. We are trying to build the house of work on the rock of wisdom. This brings us to a vital question.

Buddhism has for thousands of years provided a spiritual foundation for the daily lives of millions around the world. But does Buddhism have anything to offer us—Buddhists and non-Buddhists alike—in today's world of work? It does, and we offer it in this book. Such wisdom can inspire and instruct us in how to live a good life—a fulfilled, happy life. We offer you the teachings of the Buddha and his tradition, as well as our own application of these teachings to your work situations.

The Buddha and Buddhism

The Buddha was a human being, not a god. He compared himself to a doctor, dispensing the medicine of mindfulness—insight into our human problems, both as individuals and as groups. But more than offering insight into our problems, he taught us how to transcend them. Beginning with his own experience of enlightenment, or awakening (the word *Buddha* means "awakened one"), he created a system of thought—the Buddhist tradition—that provides helpful, practical answers to typical human situations we face in our work lives today. Buddhism is, above all, useful. It is not about pie in the sky; it is about here and now. It is not about theory; it is about *practice*. It is not just a way of thinking; it is a way of *being* and *doing*.

The Buddha was not born "Buddha"—he earned that name. He struggled with life just as we do today, and he discovered the keys to living. He sought to teach his discoveries to others, and we seek to continue his teaching by sharing it with you.

The core of the Buddha's teaching lies in his very first sermon. In it, he taught that both self-indulgence and self-mortification are useless. They do not, in the end, lead to happiness, no matter the context. He then went on to teach the four noble truths: (1) Life is full of dukkha. We suffer because we get what we don't want; we don't get what we *do* want; and, even if we do get what we want, either we can't keep it or we just worry about losing it. (2) Dukkha is caused by desire for things and attachment to things.

(3) Desire can be ended (and so dukkha can be ended!). (4) The way to end desire is by following the *eightfold noble path* of right view, right intention, right speech, right action, right livelihood, right effort, right mindfulness, and right concentration (again, see the glossary for more details).

It's easy to see how relevant some of these aspects of the path are to the workplace. Others are harder. We're here to help.

The Buddha in You (and Us)

This book is founded on the belief that the Buddha was not just a historical figure who lived 2,500 years ago. We believe that in a profound sense, the Buddha also exists within each of us at every moment. The Buddha exists in what has been called the *Buddha mind* or *Buddha nature*, the mind of the Buddha that lies sleeping within us, waiting to be awakened. We've all had moments of awakening—even if we're not Buddhists—when something has roused the Buddha mind from slumber; moments when we've lived outside our limited selves, in union with all things, flowing with the unending current of life. This liberation (Christians might call it grace) does not come when we ask for it but when we're open to it. When we think and act with this freedom, we don't just act like Buddhas, we *become* Buddhas. Not Buddh*ists*—that doesn't matter—just Buddhas. Of course, we fall back into ourselves, but this fundamental freedom remains in the moment if we can just expand into it.

In this book, we draw on a wide variety of Buddhist texts, both ancient and modern, to help you experience that expansion. The *dharma*, the teaching of the Buddha, has grown through the centuries. In this way, Buddhism is a living thing, fostered by those who seek awakening in their own lives. A contemporary haiku by a poet writing from Buddha mind is just as sacred and legitimate as an ancient scroll by a venerated monk. Each inspired writer expands the dharma in his or her own work. We humbly try to expand the dharma in ours here.

This book aims to help you be the Buddha that you already are, to find your own Buddha nature, and to allow that nature to guide you in your workaday activities. The Buddha in you is your best teacher. We believe the workplace issues and challenges we've outlined here will help you bring that Buddha to life.

A Note About Using This Book

Our book is divided into three main parts. Part 1, "Becoming a Mindful Worker," explores the Buddha's wisdom for *individuals*. Here we cover such things as how to choose right livelihood, how to be a good employee, and how to be successful. Part 2, "Cultivating Mindful Work Relationships," focuses on how to work with *other people*, including bosses, coworkers, work teams, difficult people, and customers. Part 3, "Creating a Mindful Workplace," deals with broad *organizational* topics, including policies and procedures, human resources issues, technology, work processes, and organizational problems.

If you have a specific work problem on which you'd like some guidance, just look it up in the table of contents and go straight to the answer. Of course, we can't list every possible situation in one book, but 108 issues is a pretty substantial sampling. You can also read straight through the book to get the big picture and begin to put together your own thoughts and practices for becoming more mindful and more accepting, wherever you are.

We have written for the broadest possible audience, from frontline workers to supervisors and managers to senior executives. There is wisdom and guidance here for entrepreneurs and small businesses, as well as Fortune 500 companies. Many of the ideas apply to nonprofit organizations as well as for-profit businesses. But of course, not all answers will be equally useful to all readers. Some are directed more to managers and business owners, while others are directed more to worker bees. But remember, like bees, we are all in this game of work together, so you may gain by reading answers that at first glance seem not to apply to you.

We have also written for a broad audience in terms of familiarity with Buddhist teachings. Some readers are practicing Buddhists who seek to further their understanding of and commitment to the *bodhisattva* path; other readers may not know what a bodhisattva even *is*. Some seek to practice the Buddha's teachings in every aspect of their working life; others may simply be seeking a few tips and tools to help them make it through the workday. We welcome all readers to these pages. We do not insist that you become a bodhisattva, but if you wish to do so, you can find many wonderful books that will take you deeper into this. Our book is a more applied, practical, how-to approach to workaday problems and difficulties—a Buddhist tool kit for the workplace.

The Buddha isn't here to answer our specific questions for us, but we have done our best to understand his teachings and apply them as we think *he* would. Some of these teachings are general and philosophical; others are detailed and specific. That's because some workplace problems are basic or universal, so we can point to basic and universal solutions, while other problems are more complex and require more detailed answers. The wide variety of topics addresses the wide variety of situations we face in our different jobs, different organizations, different times, and different careers.

Finally, it is important that you not accept the Buddha's teachings just because he was the Buddha. He famously told his followers to think for themselves—to question his teachings and test them against their own experience and understanding, only retaining what worked. If that was true for the Buddha, how much more so is it true for us! Test the Buddha's teachings and test this book's. Your path is unique to you, and ultimately only *you* can decide what advice is useful and what advice isn't on that path. Please take what you will, and use it as you want.

PART I

❀ Becoming a Mindful Worker

To study the Buddha way is to study the self.
—Dogen Zenji, Genjo Koan

A GREAT BEAUTY OF the Buddha's teachings is how they always return our attention to us, to our minds. Everything we feel and do is driven by mind. This means you can follow the path of awakening, no matter what anyone else around you is doing. Your awakening and growth are not contingent on others. You might find this thought frightening; you might find it liberating.

Some people want to put their faith and future in others' hands:

- "Just tell me what to do, boss, and I'll do it," they say.
- "Leaders are supposed to have the answers; that's what they get paid the big bucks for," they emphasize.
- "I just work here; I don't make the rules," they deflect.

For such people, realizing that fate, or karma, lies solely in their own hands can be upsetting—or at the very least, unsettling. Others may find the Buddha's message terrifically empowering:

- "You get out of it what you are willing to put into it," they suggest.
- "If I own the problem, I also own the solution," they point out.
- "I create my own future, through my thinking, my decisions, my actions, and my attitude," they assert.

For these people, the profoundly personal nature of mindfulness and awakening is exciting, and following its path is deeply satisfying. These are the lucky, the bodhisattvas (beings who are focused on awakening).

But most of us are not yet bodhisattvas—at least not consistently. We feel mixed emotions about the prospect and path of becoming mindful workers. Sometimes we feel great, eager to embark, devoted to continuing. At those times, we, too, are bodhisattvas. Other times, we feel discouraged, in need of guidance, spiritually inadequate. That is when we need help.

In this section, we apply the Buddha's words to many aspects of work. You may be discouraged in trying to find the right job. You may be shaky in marshaling the strength and skill that your work demands. You might be looking for new solutions to old problems. Or you might simply be looking for confirmation of the work values and attitudes you've long held. Maybe your own Buddha nature is already well awakened. Whatever your interest or need, the Buddha has wisdom for you. His example and his teaching can help you bring your spiritual life to work and bring your work to life.

In these answers, the Buddha often returns to two fundamental teachings. First, no one is inadequate. Each of us has the Buddha nature within. Second, we always have a choice. To be awake is always optional. Mindful or mindless—our decision.

🐚 Choosing Mindful Work

Creating Right Livelihood

What Are the Advantages of Mindful Work?

Since there is nothing to attain, the bodhisattva lives by
the perfection of wisdom with no hindrance in the mind;
no hindrance and therefore no fear. —The Heart Sutra

WHAT ARE THE advantages of mindful work? The Buddha would simply say they're the advantages of awakening, because mindful work brings awakening to the workplace. This is true because, fundamentally, awakening is the state of being fully aware—fully mindful, having your mind *full*—of reality. The first person to see the Buddha after he was awakened asked, "What are you?" The Buddha answered, "I am awake." Enlightenment is being awake to the reality of reality.

So the question becomes, "Reality—what's that, and why would I want to awaken to it?" And the answer is, "Reality is the interconnectedness of all things, and you want to awaken to this because it frees you from your limitations."

Awakening/enlightenment, full mindfulness of reality, is the core of Buddhism, and there is no reason why it cannot be the core of work as well. Mindful work wakes up the workplace and the world. The "perfection of wisdom" that the Heart Sutra describes is a Buddhist spiritual practice, but what does that mean? Work practice can be spiritual practice. And Buddhist spiritual practice comes down to mindfulness. So these spheres of life are not separate. And this non-separateness is not about attaining anything; it's about being there, at work or at home, without hindrance and without fear.

"Which comes first," you might ask, "mindfulness or mindful work?" Well, where are you, right now? Do the work of the moment. Take a first step. Sure, a first step is not a whole journey; nor is a first answer a whole book. Keep on.

How Do You Choose the Right Career or Job?

A bird catcher said to the Teacher, "My family's always been bird catchers. If we stop, we'll starve. But doing this [evil] work, can I still reach Buddhahood?"

The Teacher answered, "The mind goes to hell, not the body. So when you kill a bird, take your mind and kill it too. Doing this, you can reach Buddhahood." —Suzuki Shosan, Roankyo

A LMOST EVERYONE AT one time or another has asked, "How do I find the right career, the right job, where I will be fulfilled and happy?" If you are seeking to learn from the Buddha's teachings, this question is especially important, because part of the very core of Buddhism, the *eightfold noble path*, is right livelihood. Simply put, that means doing work that helps, rather than harms, all living things. As the Buddha brought work into the spiritual life, he brought spirituality into work life. Right livelihood is being the Buddha at work.

For many people, this is a serious problem. What if you work for a company that makes instruments of destruction? What if you work for an organization whose fundamental mission is not aligned with your own values? Can you still do mindful work? Can you still pursue right livelihood?

The Zen teacher Suzuki's answer here is very interesting. He taught that we should try hard never to harm other living things, and yet he reconciles enlightenment with bird catching. How can this be? The key issue, it seems, is not so much what your body is doing but what your mind is doing. Of course, the mind and the body are intimately connected, and one often follows the other in day-to-day life. But this need not always be so. It is possible to have the body engaged in one activity and the mind focused on something else. Here, he advises the bird catcher to kill the bird if he absolutely must (he recognizes that people have to make a living), while keeping the mind not on killing the bird (which would be wrong livelihood) but on killing the mind—that is, killing desire and attachment. A creative solution, and one that acknowledges the power of our environment over us. There are times when we cause harm without meaning to.

Of course, the Buddha would never accept this as a long-term solution. He would encourage the bird catcher to change jobs if he could. Bird catching simply is not right livelihood. But perhaps for the time being, there is no choice. You must feed yourself and your family, and this means you must make a living in a compromised fashion. You'll simply have to work that much harder to keep your mind pure until you can find work that *is* right livelihood.

You can pursue enlightenment no matter what job you have, and you can often transform your boring or unfulfilling work into mindful work by changing how you *think* about your work, by changing your spirit. You can be a garbage collector, in the spirit of love and service, and be well on your way to Buddhahood. There's no question that garbage collecting is right livelihood, while a creative and high-paying position in a corrupt and greedy field is not. Whatever your job is, start there; adopt the right mind and take that first step on the path. Yes, the path may lead you to change careers, but the Buddha does not demand that you harm yourself in doing so. In the end, only a career that helps will make you truly fulfilled.

What Does It Mean to Be a Great Employee?

A good employee serves her employer in five ways: by getting up and starting work before her; by stopping after her; by taking from her employer only what is given; by striving to do her work well; and by upholding her employer's name. —Digha Nikaya 31

IF YOU'RE WONDERING what you can do to endear yourself to the boss, to be a great employee, the Buddha has some words of wisdom for you. Get back to basics. Forget about kissing up—no one is impressed by that. To be a great employee, start by doing great work. Here are the five suggestions that the Buddha gave:

1. Get up and start work before your boss. It never hurts to arrive at work a little bit early; you will be calm and collected as you start your day.

2. Stop work after your boss does: being willing to stay a little longer to tie up loose ends or to help a coworker is a great way to show that you are willing to go the extra mile. And, so often, this quieter time is the most productive in the day.

3. Take from your employer only what is given. Not taking what is not ours is one of the five basic Buddhist precepts. It may seem harmless to take home that pencil or that wrench or some other little thing, but it really *is* stealing, and it's the first step on a long downward spiral. Everyone may do it, but you don't want to be just like everyone, do you? You want to be authentically you.

4. Strive to do your work well. This may seem obvious, but many people do just enough work to get by . . . and then wonder why they aren't doing better in their careers. Don't waste time on scheming or daydreaming; the Buddha always focused on effort. The bottom line: above all else, do great work!

5. Uphold your employer's name. To many people you meet, you *are* your organization. Whether you are on the job or off, speak well of your employer and represent them well in the community; it will come back to reward you in surprising ways.

What does it take to be a great employee? You can always add more things to this list, of course, but the Buddha lays it out plain: start with the basics.

Can You Have Self-Esteem and Still Be Buddha?

As a solid rock doesn't quaver in the wind,
So the wise are moved by neither praise nor blame.
—Dhammapada 81

YOU MAY HAVE heard that the Buddha denied the existence of the self. Let's be clear: the Buddha never denied that we experience the world and our lives through a sense of self. This self matters and needs attention. What the Buddha denied was that this self is *enduring*. Our selves arise and pass away; they exist in their relationships and experiences, and these are constantly changing.

The Buddha respects the need for self-esteem. The self in this world needs to feel positive about itself. He warns you not to be swayed by other people's opinion of you or your work. You know when you have done your best work, and you are the best person to judge your own actions. Do not give away your self-confidence by letting others' opinions determine whether you feel good or bad about yourself. If you let others' praise or criticism affect your sense of self-worth, you will forever be a slave to public opinion. In a sense, what they think of you is none of your business. Does a rock care what the wind thinks of it? A rock just goes on doing its thing. So do Buddhas. So can you.

It is a truism that people who feel good about themselves produce good results. It is also true that people who produce good results feel good about themselves. Which comes first, the self-esteem or the good results?

The Buddha would tell us it doesn't matter which comes first. If you feel good about yourself, chances are, you are already producing good results. If you don't feel good about yourself, try producing good results and see how your self-esteem improves. Instead of the contemporary "power of positive thinking," Buddhism emphasizes the "power of positive *doing*." Get into action, and see how it improves your mood, sometimes immediately. Action alleviates anxiety. It also helps elevate self-esteem and can even lighten depression. So, if your self-esteem isn't all you'd like it to be, get your butt in gear. Perhaps the Buddha would phrase it differently, but no less bluntly. Act in the awareness of the rightness of action, even if you don't feel positive. In this scenario, thinking will follow acting.

Dealing with Distractions

Reaching for the silence
he hears
every single sound.
—Steven Sanfield, "A Poem for Those of You
  Who Are Sometimes Troubled by Barking Dogs
  and Low Flying Jets," in *American Zen*[1]

THE POET STEVE SANFIELD is not a psychologist, but he is a Buddhist, and he is certainly onto the irony of the vexed relationship between concentration and distraction.

If we are so easily distracted, what can we do to focus in order to see projects through to completion? The Buddha advises us to train our minds, specifically through meditation and other forms of spiritual discipline. Having a trained mind is good because it lets us focus on the important things. A trained mind brings ease because it is uncluttered. We no longer feel the anxiety of the *monkey mind*, chattering endlessly, or hear the thousand sounds that assail us. We cannot stop up our ears, but we can stop—or at least calm—the mind.

How? Take up a spiritual practice. Whether this is a martial art like aikido, a meditation practice like zazen or Transcendental Meditation (TM), a physical discipline like hatha yoga, a devotional practice like reciting scripture or prayer, or even a complex game like chess is not important—just practice *something*. It can even be simple mindfulness while you eat or drive or brush your teeth. Practice trains the mind, and a trained mind is a good thing. Your best choice is to look around and pick something you *like*. If you train in a way you like, you'll simply *do* it more. As you do, your mind will focus better and longer.

Within the confines of this book, we can't train your mind for you, but here's one suggestion for beginners: when you feel distracted or angry or sleepy, acknowledge it; don't deny it. That begins the training: react to the negative with the positive. Now, strengthen the positive by bringing the mind back to breathing. Stop moving; relax. Take a deep breath. Don't think; just feel the breath. Don't try to breathe in any special way; just breathe naturally and let your mind rest in that breathing. You can count your breaths if it helps you. Count to ten. Let the myriad things rest. Now come back to the moment. You have trained yourself to find strength in the face of distraction. Take the strength of that focus on the breath and apply it to your task.

✿ Practical Enlightenment

Chop Wood, Carry Water

Why Should I Have Beginner's Mind?

If your mind is empty, it is always ready for anything;
it is open to everything. In the beginner's mind there are
many possibilities; in the expert's mind there are few.
—Shunryu Suzuki, *Zen Mind, Beginner's Mind*[1]

MOST PEOPLE THINK it is important to have a lot of knowledge, and they go to great lengths to try to impress others with how much they know. In this deservedly famous passage, Suzuki Roshi pointedly emphasized the limitations of such an attitude toward knowledge and experience in the spiritual life. It is the same in business life. In order to understand what my customers want and need, I must cultivate a beginner's mind. For them to teach me, I have to clear space to learn.

There's an old Zen story of a professor who visits a renowned Zen master and, instead of learning, goes on about what he himself knows. The master fills the professor's cup of tea—and keeps on pouring. When the professor asks what the master is doing, the master tells him, "Like this cup, you are full. How can I teach you Zen unless you first empty your cup?"

If you want to open yourself to Suzuki's "many possibilities," abandon preconceptions; ask thoughtful questions; and above all, listen and learn. This is true whether approaching a new employee, a new task, a new career, or a new challenge in the marketplace. There are times when the smartest businesspeople put aside what they think they know and adopt beginner's mind.

How Can You Use Your Buddha Mind to Establish Priorities?

The wise person, who hurries when it's time to hurry, and
who slows his pace down when slowness is the thing, is deeply
happy because he's got priorities in line. —Theragatha 161

PETER DRUCKER, the grandfather of today's management consultants and business thinkers, says the challenge of the modern manager is that he knows there are ten things needing to be done, but he has time to do only six. He's got to pick the right six to do, and then go home at night and not worry about the four he had to let go.

The Buddha would tell us that Drucker's statement applies to everyone, not just managers. We work in fast motion, and there are many demands on our time. The task is not to somehow find more time but rather to make the most of the time we have. Our real challenge is not short time but effective prioritization.

We must each choose what is most important to our happiness and to our success, in life and in work. Time-management experts offer a variety of useful tools and techniques. Some examples: Use an A, B, C ranking to sort projects and tasks into categories; then do the A-priority things first, B-priority things next, and C-priority things only if you have time left over. Or, distinguish between urgent and important, and then do things that are both urgent and important first, followed by those that are important but not urgent; items that are not important and not urgent—don't do them.

If you're having trouble prioritizing your work, ask someone to help you—your boss or a trusted coworker. Often, we can see what others need to do more clearly than we can see what we need to do, so getting another's perspective can be a wise move. Wise workers know how to tap into the wisdom of others.

Once we have made our choices, our daily actions follow from them. Instead of racing around frantically, treating everything like an emergency, we hurry when it is appropriate, and we slow down when that is appropriate. This is harder than it sounds. We make different choices and have different insights in these different speed modes. We need to use both in mindful work.

How Does Mindfulness Help with Time Management?

Yunmen addressed his monks and said, "I do not ask about before the 15th of the month; tell me about after the 15th." Nobody said anything, so he answered himself: "Every day is a good day."
—The Blue Cliff Record, case 6

ZEN TEACHER YUNMEN does not ask his people about the past; he knows the past is gone and there is nothing anyone can do about it. Yet he is not asking about the future, either, for he also knows that no one can predict the future. He is testing to see if they are worrying uselessly about time, past or future. He is asking about *now*, the moment of awakening. Concerned and perplexed, the monks do not answer.

Perhaps we can do better. Yunmen is trying to teach them (and us) that it is pointless to expend energy lamenting the past or worrying about the future when we cannot control either one. It is pointless to divide up our years and days, living as if we were calendars. From a pure Zen perspective, there *is* no future or past. We're not like calendars—we're more like clocks. We tell the time as it happens. Our hands are always pointing to *now*. There is no 15th, nor any day before or after. All we really have to work with is today, and today is a good day.

If the Buddha told us to "have a nice day," he would not be making small talk; he would be challenging us to *do* it. The heart of effective time management was, is, and will be mindfulness of this moment.

Does the Buddha Have Any Wisdom about Procrastination?

"It's too cold, too hot, too late."
With excuses like these,
People shirk their work,
And the moment passes them by.
—Theragatha 231

W HO AMONG US isn't guilty of procrastination? It's so seductive and seems so harmless when we succumb to it. "Oh, I'll get to that project later. I don't have time to do it now." "Who can work in this heat?" "I'll make those phone calls tomorrow. It's too late in the day; I'm sure everyone's already gone home." "I'll just take care of these little things first and save the big one for when I have a bigger chunk of time." Sure, uh-huh. Some of these reasons may even hold a grain of truth. Unfortunately, all too many times, the window of opportunity closes, and we kick ourselves (or someone else kicks us) for having missed our chance.

The wise person knows the dangers of procrastination and resists the siren song that tells her to put off 'til tomorrow. Put things off even once, and you begin to establish a pattern flowing from your inner resistance. If others, feeling similarly, follow your lead, you've created a whole culture of procrastination. Your team begins to lag behind.

In place of this, the wise person looks directly into her procrastination and sees the resistance underlying it. She knows that resistance is not only normal but valuable: she asks where resistance comes from, knowing she will learn something vital about herself and her relation to the work at hand. She may enlist the help of others in overcoming her resistance: she asks her coach or mentor for help, or she teams up with an action buddy—someone she can call on whenever she needs support in tackling something she's having trouble doing. She learns and then she acts, making the moment count. Acting mindfully in the moment, we stay ahead of the curve and are able to set the terms; we flow with the Tao (Chinese for the "way," the movement of all things). If the Buddha spoke Latin, he might have said, "Carpe diem!"

What Can You Do about Too Much E-mail?

It is completely open,
Nothing wanting, nothing extra.
Hold or reject and
You lose its thusness.
   —Sengcan, "Trusting in Mind"

THE THIRD ZEN Ancestor, Sengcan, describes the great way, the path of the sages. No "too much" here. It is we who create categories such as "too much" and "too little." In the Buddha mind there is only what is—no evaluations of excess or insufficiency—and since there are no evaluations, there is also no distress caused by judgments and assessments, nothing wanting and nothing extra.

This may sound crazy to the modern working person's mind, brimming with judgments, evaluations, and criticisms. Our problem is, we tell ourselves (and each other) stories about how things "should" be and then get upset because things don't occur as we prefer. Our "shoulds" and "oughts" cause us to suffer. We may object, "This isn't the life I ordered," but things in our lives are not under our command. Life occurs on life's terms—not on yours, not on mine. The Buddha mind surveys your e-mail, the piles of paper on your desk, the work in your briefcase, and simply says, "Thus." The Buddha mind does not suffer, because it has no preconceived ideas about the volume of e-mail . . . or anything else. Without suffering, we are free to tackle the e-mail itself without the distraction of holding on to our imaging reality or rejecting our actual reality. We are free to find the ease of openness.

How Can We Avoid Wasting Time in Cyberspace?

The Web site you seek
cannot be located, but
endless others exist.
—Joy Rothke, in "Haiku Error Messages,"
from 21st Century Challenge #4, Salon.com

THE BUDDHA WOULD profoundly appreciate the infinite world of cyberspace and its endless possibilities. He would see in it a reflection of the infinite universe around us: vast, complex, marvelous to behold, each tiny piece of the great Web potentially linked to every other. Disordered, ceaselessly changing, vulnerable to attack, finally indestructible, the Web indeed reflects our world.

And just *because* it reflects our world, we can get lost in it. We succumb to the lure of following just one more link, checking out just one more site. Here are a few tips for breaking this cycle: First, no personal Web activity at work. In fact, this is not a tip; this is a rule. Second, set a timer on surfing. You know the expression "There's an app for that"? Well, there are several. Use one. Third, every 15 minutes or so, ask yourself, "What's the best use of my time, right now?" Answer honestly. (You can use this tip all day, not just online.) Finally, whenever you even wonder if being online is productive, that's your cue to get up and walk away from your computer.

Just as we can never satisfy our endless desire for worldly pleasures, so can we never satisfy our endless desire for virtual pleasures. The Web site you seek cannot be located. You can use your senses to search for pleasure or you can use search engines, but your satisfaction will come only when you search within and find no one to satisfy. Luckily, though the Web site cannot be located, neither can the user.

How Can You Do Your Job of Selling— without Selling Out?

The great cloud rains down on all beings,
whether their nature is superior or inferior.
—Lotus Sutra 5

SALESPEOPLE ARE THE rainmakers for their companies. Rainmakers do their magic dance, bringing nourishing rain to grow their businesses. It is not for them to judge but to serve.

Essential to any effective rainmaker's dance are the attention, interest, and kindness he shows his customers. If he is wise and compassionate (remember that these are the two great virtues of Buddhism), he doesn't make sales calls—he makes service calls. He knows that his primary job is to help his customers become more successful—his job is to provide what his customers need. When he rains kindness on his customer, his customer rains appreciation in the form of money on the rainmaker and his company. In this valuesdriven business model, serving others is fundamental, and money is the by-product of providing service.

A rainmaker not in his right mind—that is, his Buddha mind—has lost sight of the essence of business. Such a salesperson thinks the goal is getting what he can from his customers; he has made money his object of worship and will go to any lengths to get it. Such a rainmaker has sold his soul for success, but he doesn't really succeed at all. Customers are smart, and sooner or later they will realize that he isn't interested in serving them at all; he is interested simply in what he can get from them. His customers are likely to switch vendors when they can, preferring to do business with a salesperson who genuinely cares about their needs.

A rainmaker who is wise and compassionate embodies those virtues even in the act of selling. Does that seem odd? Only because we have falsely divorced virtue from the market. In fact, selling goods or services that you know are useful is wise. Selling them to people who can genuinely benefit from them is compassionate. This works the same way as right speech, which communicates something true and useful at the right time. Here we have right sales, selling something harmless and useful to the right person. This is the basis of a Buddhist economy.

What Would the Buddha Tell Us about Handling a Highly Distasteful Job?

The Buddha said if we really need to,
We have to do some really nasty things.
But never just because someone has asked.
—The Precious Jewel of the Teaching 12,
quoting the Ratnavali

SOMETIMES WE ARE asked to do things at work that we really don't want to do. Somebody has to do the grunt work, and sometimes that somebody is you. The distasteful task might be a special project, or it might be part of your regular duties. Distasteful jobs can include firing people, cutting budgets, dealing with conflicts, cleaning up messes, working with difficult circumstances and/or difficult people. These jobs can be physically nasty, emotionally nasty, morally nasty; every organization has its share of nasty jobs and unpleasant duties that someone has to do.

But nasty jobs raise an interesting question for people following the wisdom of the Buddha. He says that just because you are asked to do such a job does not mean you necessarily have to do it. What, is he crazy? How can you *not* do a nasty job you are asked to do at work? What will your boss say?

We all need to shoulder responsibility, and we all have to do our share of nasty jobs, but we do not have to do them *all,* and we do not have to do them just because someone asks us. The Buddha tells you to ask, "Is this something I really need to do?" Your answer to that question will grow from your answers to the question's several dimensions: "Does this job genuinely need to be done? Am I the best person in the organization to do this job? Is doing this job a test I need to pass?" And finally, perhaps the most important question: "Can I learn from the process of doing this job?"

If you can learn from a nasty job, you do need to do it. If the nasty job seems pointless and you see no redeeming aspects to it whatsoever, you might want to have a conversation with your boss and see if you can negotiate some other arrangement. Easier said than done, granted, but the practice of having such a discussion with your boss can be a powerful learning experience in itself. It just may be that the nasty task is not the only learning experience—how you think about and respond to the nasty task may be the *real* learning opportunity.

🦋 Quality of Work Life

The Middle Way at Work

Juyi asked, "What is the profound point of the Buddhadharma?"
Daolin answered, "Refraining from harmful action and practicing helpful action."
Juyi retorted, "Bah, even a three year old could say that!"
Daolin replied, "A three year old could say it, but not even an eighty year old can practice it!"
—Dogen Zenji, Shoaku Makusa

THE HUMAN MIND is a thicket, full of impediments to following the path. Even when we know perfectly well what to do, we often don't do it. Some call this fear of success; others call it fear of failure; still others say the problem is perfectionism. Who knows the truth? Human beings have been trying to understand themselves and their failures for millennia.

Most of us know what's good for us, but we don't do it. As the apostle Paul wrote, "I do not understand myself. For what I want to do, I do not do. But what I hate, I do." Since the ways of the "I" are so difficult to understand, one wise thing you can do is enlist the support of others in your efforts. Everyone needs a team, a *sangha*, a community—we are social animals who do better when surrounded by others committed to our well-being. Your team might include trusted friends, work colleagues, professional helpers such as therapists and life coaches, advisors such as financial planners and business managers, mentors, and career coaches. Some people hold regular meetings of their support groups—referring to them as mastermind groups or success teams. No one can build a successful life for you, but you can't do it alone.

Remember, though, your support team supports; it doesn't do the work. "You must walk; Buddhas just show the path" (Dhammapada 276). For most of us, the wisest thing we can do is spend time in meditation, getting acquainted with our troublesome self. The more we become aware of the deviousness of our mind, the more we acknowledge the problem. And the more we accept the problem, the more power we gain to do what that three-year-old knows we should do.

How Can You Deal with Discouragement at Work?

Once, during a meditation retreat, a student said to the zen teacher Soen Nakagawa, "I am very discouraged. What should I do?" Soen replied, "Encourage others." This is zen thinking.
—Philip Toshio Sudo, *Zen Computer*[1]

PHILIP TOSHIO SUDO gives us a beautiful vignette from the work of a beloved Zen teacher. It exemplifies Zen thinking by turning away from the eternal troubles of the self and out toward the eternal possibilities of helping others.

Yes, we know this is hard to do. And we know it is hardest to do exactly when you are most burdened by your own discouragement. But that is what is so remarkable about doing it anyway. You feel better. You may think you have nothing left, nothing to give. But when you have no encouragement for yourself, you will be surprised as you discover how you can still find great compassion for others. When your own trouble is right at the surface, you will see their troubles so much more clearly. Lose yourself in helping them. As soon as you do, your own troubles are over.

Will they return? *Of course* they'll return. Troubles come and troubles go; that is the way of things. But it's all right, because in helping others, you'll find that you have helped yourself. It's a miracle.

How Can You Handle Rumors and Gossip at Work?

What is right speech? Abstaining from lying,
divisive speech, abusive speech, and idle chatter.
—Samyutta Nikaya 45.8

THE BUDDHA DID not indulge in rumors or gossip. Right speech forms part of the eightfold path because speech has great power. To follow the Buddha's path, we must not engage in talk that divides people, talk that criticizes people behind their backs, or talk that is just chatter to kill time. Are rumors and gossip any of these? They're all of these.

The Buddha knows you don't mean ill to people when you talk about what's going on with a coworker or another department. You're simply curious, or amused, or disapproving of someone else. But this idle speculation and chatting is almost always destructive. Things get repeated and *always* get distorted in the repeating. By the time a comment has made the full circuit on the company grapevine, it has been totally changed and is completely inaccurate (if it was ever accurate at all).

Trust is impossible in such an environment. Gossip and rumors set an organizational tone in which everyone feels unsafe. People communicate warily because they worry about what others are saying behind their backs. Both gossip and the worry it creates suck up time that could be spent solving problems, cultivating new ideas, or exploring new markets. Productivity and profitability are bound to suffer. So, when we indulge in gossip or rumors, we are hurting not only our organization but also our own future, by undermining the strength of our enterprise.

The Company You Keep

*Being friends, companions, and colleagues with admirable people
is actually the whole of the noble life. The monk who has the
good and virtuous as friends, companions, and colleagues will
stay on the eightfold path.* —Samyutta Nikaya 45.2

MANY MOTHERS CAUTION their children not to associate
with bullies, troublemakers, and those who are up to no
good: "You're judged by the company you keep." True, others
will think well of you when they see you with good people. But
there is an even more compelling reason to choose your friends
and colleagues wisely: admirable people will move you to become
a better person.

When the Buddha said these words we quote, he was responding to someone saying that being with admirable people
was half of the noble life. The Buddha contradicted him: it's *all*
of the noble life.

If you want to cultivate patience and kindness, hang around
with patient, kind people. If you want to have more integrity,
spend time with those who embody it. Surround yourself with
people actively contributing to their organizations and to the
world. If you want right livelihood, seek out people who are doing
what you'd like to do. Note that we're suggesting one possible
solution to mistrust in the workplace. *This* is where you belong.
If you can't create trust in your workplace, find another.

How Can You Achieve Balance between Your Work and Personal Life?

Healthy tension is the natural complementarity of structure and inspiration, responsibility and personal fulfillment, discipline and freedom, authority and egalitarianism, tradition and relevance, male and female, form and void, life and nonexistence. Neglect one side of the pair, and it will turn around and bite.

—Robert Aitken, *Encouraging Words*[2]

I S LIFE AN either/or proposition, or is it both/and? We live on a continuum of polarities: work versus play, community versus individuality, male versus female, young versus old, task versus relationship, and so on. We live in the dialectical tension between these polar opposites, being pulled in two directions at once. The Buddha understood this, and Aitken Roshi reminds us that this is not just unavoidable: it is *healthy*.

We must attend to both ends of these polarities. We must spend time alone as well as time in community; we must pay attention to relationships as well as tasks; we must find time for work and for play. Those of us who choose one end of a continuum while ignoring the other never do so successfully, for the neglected end will come back to bite us. If we have too much freedom, we lack the structure and discipline we need to improve ourselves; yet if we have too much structure, we become rigid and stifled with no freedom for inspiration and innovation.

So it is with life inside and outside of work. As a scale fulfills its function when its sides are equally balanced, so we humans function best when we balance work life and personal life—we can be loose, relaxed, capable of movement, just, and fair. This is the Buddha's middle way.

What Are the Costs and Benefits of Integrity and Wisdom?

Life is easy for the shameless, cunning,
Corrupt, brazen, nasty, and betraying.
But for one who's honest and insightful,
Trying to pursue purity, it's hard.
—Dhammapada 244–245

W HY DO SO few people follow the path of mindful work? Because it's hard. The Buddha levels with us. Living a life of integrity is hard work. Following the path of spiritual growth is hard work. Awakening and staying mindful in each moment requires constant honesty. It's exhausting (though sometimes also exhilarating), but it expands through all your relations and creates a lasting legacy. The benefits of integrity and wisdom compound over time.

It's easier to just give in to your worst impulses and let the least common denominator of the workplace drive you. Following a spiritual path at work is like trying to maintain a meticulously clean house while still living in it . . . along with a pack of teenagers! It takes time, attention, and energy. Living in a laid-back, messy house is much easier in the short run. Spend your energy on momentary and trivial pursuits; don't invest in the future. The teenagers will agree. That tells you something.

You have to look at the costs and benefits in the long run as well. It's there you'll find that even though the cost of integrity is hard work, the price of giving in is your integrity itself. Without your integrity, you are merely a succession of meaningless moments, always vanishing. This is too high a price to pay. Still, it's your choice. There is a cost and a payoff to living a mindful life, and there is a cost and a payoff to living a foolish life. The Buddha would tell you to do the math and then decide.

❀ Being Successful

How Do You Define Success?

How Do Buddhas Achieve Their Goals?

He constantly abandons useless mindsets and cultivates useful mindsets. He is resolute and concentrated in his effort. He never abandons his efforts toward achieving useful mindsets.

—Anguttara Nikaya 5.53

THE BUDDHA IS the spiritual father to some of today's "success writers" whose best sellers teach us how to manifest our dreams and achieve our goals. These authors are tapping into what the Buddha knew 2,500 years ago: that the mind has immense power, if only its owner would use it well. The Buddha urges us to keep laserlike focus (okay, they didn't have lasers in the Buddha's day; he called it "one-pointed mind") on our vision or objective—to be unwavering in our concentration. A man with a mission does not dissipate and waste energy on useless distractions. Nor does he cling to negative mind-sets. Sometimes those mind-sets have allure (we all know the twisted pleasures of holding a grudge or feeling put-upon), but never are they useful.

The Buddha teaches us that focusing attention on the desired goal and letting go of internal hindrances are all that is required for success. Set your mind toward your goals. Evaluate what are useful mind-sets for you. Stick to them. Do not be distracted by useless mind-sets. Never abandon your effort!

What Would the Buddha Say about Multitasking?

When the mind is composed, this is concentration.
If you cling to externals, the mind is distracted and confused.
If you are unattached to externals, then the mind is composed.
—Huineng, The Platform Sutra

FOR MANY YEARS, busy people have prided themselves on their multitasking ability—their skill at doing several things at once and so getting more done than other folks. Only one problem: in the last few years, psychologists and productivity experts have discovered that multitasking isn't very effective on the job. Mistakes get made, details overlooked; things fall between the cracks. Productivity and quality standards both suffer. Studies support what the Buddha taught 2,500 years ago—that concentration beats dividing one's attention and juggling many projects simultaneously. When our attention and energy are scattered, our work suffers. Very often our health also suffers, from the pressure of too many projects, too many deadlines, too much stress.

The Buddha would advise prioritizing our projects so that we tackle the most important ones first, rather than jumping back and forth between them. Our monkey mind (to use the ancient Buddhist term) naturally prefers to scatter our attention hither and yon, but the whole purpose of Buddhist practice is to tame the mind, to calm the monkey in our head, and to be fully present to what we are doing in each and every moment.

The Buddha would say, "Do less, and do better." The devil is in the details; if we're busy multitasking, we're not concentrating on the important details that are going to come back to bite us in the butt later on.

What Would the Buddha Teach Us about Finding the "Right" Answer to a Problem?

If you claim a position, you don't have the correct view.
—The V Dalai Lama, *The Graded Stages of the Path: Personal Instructions from Manjushri*

THE ANSWER TO our question is paradoxical: There *is* no one right answer ("correct view") to a problem or situation. As soon as we think we have the right answer, we are mistaken. But more deeply, it's not the answer that is mistaken—the mistake happens inside *us*, when we think we can definitively find a permanent answer. Since everything in life is always changing, the correct view today might be incorrect tomorrow. The right answer to a problem changes from day to day, because the problem itself is always changing. And there's more: Things change not just over time but over distance. The problem is different for others—even right now—than it is for you. Different problem, different answer.

Jean Kerr, the playwright, has said, "If you can keep your head about you when all about you are losing theirs, it's just possible you haven't grasped the situation." Wise words. Feeling anxious or unsettled is understandable when things are changing as fast as they are. No one person can stay on top of things all the time. Nor are "things" the same for different people.

Frustrating, isn't it? We humans want so very much to comfort ourselves with absolutes, to be reassured that we have the right answer. But if the Buddha is correct, and all is changing, we have to live with the anxiety and uncertainty this brings. It's a choice: we can put ourselves to sleep by clinging to absolutes ("This is the only right way"), or we can wake up and see that we must be limber and flexible, always becoming, always changing, and always needing to find changing answers to changing problems.

Would the Buddha Admit His Mistakes?

All the evil karma created by me from of old,
on account of my beginningless greed, hatred and ignorance,
born of my deeds, words and thoughts,
I now confess openly and fully.

—Zen Gatha of Purification

CONFESSION IS GOOD for the soul—or, for hard-core Buddhists, the absence of soul. Either way, confession requires honesty and humility, and we need both.

Admitting that you were wrong, or you made a mistake, is the first important step to improvement—both self-improvement and improvement on any work project. People who never admit mistakes never get to learn from them. They are doomed to keep repeating them until someone *else* discovers them. People who admit mistakes are already on their way to making fewer of them in the future. Good bosses know this. They know that *everyone* makes mistakes, and so they trust people who admit them. That's how to build working relationships. And good employees know this as well, and they 'fess up when they've made mistakes so that they can learn.

Look at what is happening in this verse: purification. Not only does admitting mistakes begin the process of learning from them, but also it begins the process of correcting them, of purifying ourselves of them. When we repeat the verse of purification, we admit our tainted past, but in admitting that taint, we also acknowledge that we see it from a better perspective. Seeing our greed, hatred, and ignorance, we also see our generosity, love, and wisdom. Admitting our mistakes is also admitting our potential greatness.

Will Being Buddha at Work Help You to Get Promoted?

High rank depends on circumstances; is only gained through effort; yet is effortlessly lost. It does not lead to contentment or happiness, still less to peace of mind. —Jatakamala 8.53

THE BUDDHA DID not work for promotions, and neither should you. Bucking for a promotion is simply your ego grasping for attention and status. Getting that promotion is not going to make your life great, and it's not going to be permanent, given today's rapid pace of change. A promotion comes with circumstances, and circumstances can take it away. No, the ultimate destination of the Buddhist path is not the top of the organizational ladder. The Buddha wouldn't do anything special to get promoted.

Paradoxically, the Buddha got promoted all the time. He had no problem with that. The Buddha was a respected aristocrat, then a venerated ascetic with followers, and ultimately the head of a whole religion. He was not afraid of rising to the top, and neither should you be. It's just that he never cared about rank or promotion. Instead, he cared about—he was utterly committed to—doing his work with brilliance. The Buddha understood that getting promoted is a happy side effect of doing excellent work. If your work speaks for itself, don't interrupt.

Where does that leave you on the career ladder? Here's the thing: reaching the top isn't as important as you think. What is going to give you contentment, happiness, and peace of mind is what gave those things to the Buddha: deep insight into the wonderful interdependence of things, the opportunity to make a contribution to your organization, and the chance to use your skills fully. When you do your very best work—when you're a Buddha—perhaps you'll even get promoted.

How Should Mindful People Celebrate Their Accomplishments?

When my success is talked about at work,
I'm quick to have everyone jump in.
But when it's others getting compliments,
I just don't feel like joining in the fun.
—Bodhicharyavatara 6.79

WE'RE SO HAPPY to revel in our own successes that we think everyone should just join right in. But the monk Shantideva (author of the insightful Bodhicharyavatara) notes how slow we are to join in celebrating the success of others. We pretend to be happy, but we feel resentful inside. With our bosses in particular, we often revert to childish attitudes, wanting to be Daddy's favorite, and resenting the praise and attention that Daddy/boss lavishes on coworkers/siblings. Of course, we would never admit this out loud, but we feel it. We are like greedy children, fearful that we won't get our share of the good stuff.

The Buddha would point out that, once again, we are succumbing to the illusion that we are separate from one another; our misperception leads us to resent others' success. "If the pinkie successfully removed the wax from your ear, the index finger wouldn't be resentful, would it?" the Buddha might ask us with a smile. Businesses ought to be as cooperative as hands. There is plenty of success to go around, and each person has the opportunity to be successful in his or her own way. How much happier we are when we celebrate everyone's successes as our own! And how much nicer we are to be with. Bosses notice *that*, too.

Does Success Lead to Happiness, or Does Happiness Lead to Success?

Whether we are rich or poor, educated or uneducated,
whatever our nationality, color, social status, or ideology
may be, the purpose of our lives is to be happy.
—The XIV Dalai Lama, in *The Spirit of Tibet,*
Vision for Human Liberation[1]

ALL GREAT SPIRITUAL teachers throughout history have delivered the same message: The best things in life aren't things. It is fine to enjoy money, achievement, promotions, applause, acclaim, and worldly success—just don't confuse them with happiness. True happiness is not to be had with a big paycheck or moving into the corner office. There will always be people with bigger paychecks or more prestigious offices. If you define happiness as "getting the best," you define yourself as an unhappy person. And the longer you practice your definition, the more consistently you'll be unhappy. This is true even if the things you want are good things or inner achievements. What if the Dalai Lama had decided he'd be happy once he succeeded in freeing Tibet? Let's see . . . That famous smile? Gone. The Nobel Peace Prize? Too depressed to do the work that earned it. The pride, the humbleness, the resilience, he has shared with his people and all the world in his 50 years of exile? Sorry, you can't expect a man frustrated for so long to be any of those things!

But he *is* those things, and he *did* win the Nobel Prize, and, though Tibet remains oppressed, he is *still smiling*. Why? Because true happiness comes not from external success but from the internal peace of feeling your life aligned with your values and beliefs. It comes from serving others without attachment to reward or success. It comes from being who we want to be. If happiness is the purpose of our lives, it can come only in our acts, living those lives authentically as ourselves.

Money and Happiness

What's the Connection?

Did the Buddha Teach That Money Is "the Root of All Evil"?

> MANJUSHRI: *What is the root of good and evil?*
> VIMALAKIRTI: *Physicality is the root of good and evil.*
> MANJUSHRI: *What is the root of physicality?*
> VIMALAKIRTI: *Desire is the root of physicality.*
> MANJUSHRI: *What is the root of desire?*
> VIMALAKIRTI: *The false self is the root of desire.*
> MANJUSHRI: *What is the root of the false self?*
> VIMALAKIRTI: *Ignorance is the root of the false self.*
> MANJUSHRI: *What is the root of ignorance?*
> VIMALAKIRTI: *Emptiness.*
> MANJUSHRI: *What is the root of emptiness?*
> VIMALAKIRTI: *When something is empty, what root can it have?*
> *So all things grow from an empty root.*
>
> —Vimalakirtinirdesha Sutra 7

THIS DIALOGUE BETWEEN two awakened beings brings out our real relationship with money. It evokes St. Paul's statement in the Bible, that love of money is the root of all evil. But the Buddhist teaching goes deeper. Our desire for money goes beyond the nature of money, even beyond the nature of desire itself. It points to the nature of all things.

Manjushri, the bodhisattva of wisdom, begins with a question asked all over the world: What is the root of all evil? The great householder bodhisattva, Vimalakirti, answers right away that not greed, not money, but focus on physicality is the root. In this, the Buddha teaches something slightly different from, but not incompatible with, what Jesus taught. Money, even loving it, is not intrinsically evil. Instead, evil comes from our delusion that the physical world is fundamental. Money responds to and perpetuates this delusion that the physical will satisfy us. In a way, money is the ultimate empty thing: something appearing huge but in fact entirely hollow. It acts to entrap us in pleasures that are themselves empty. We—both individuals and organizations—keep score with money. We measure success with money, so our earnings and our economies must always grow. Yet this never-ending quest can never be fulfilled.

This entrapment in the physical arises from our desires, our unquenchable yearnings, brought on by our ignorant belief in our selves as separate beings. In reality, our selves, and all things, are open or empty or hollow. These words express the Sanskrit *shunya*, which means having no significance or essence in and of itself. Instead, things are significant in their connections to everything else. *Shunya* means not separate, never alone. It means interfused and interdependent with all other beings, all other things. And it's how we are.

This has profound implications for our relationship with money. If this is how things really are, money distracts us from what will genuinely give us happiness: the pleasure of experiencing the whole world. The whole world is available right now, for free. You don't need money; you need freedom from desire. You also don't need to avoid money. Money only hurts you if you let it. But unless you are very wise and wonderfully self-aware, be careful that you don't start looking to money for fulfillment it can never bring. The best things in life aren't things.

Is It Okay to Have Personal Wealth?

*When a person of integrity becomes wealthy, he provides pleasures
and satisfactions for himself, for his parents, for his wife and children,
for his underlings, and for his friends. He makes offerings to priests
and holy persons, offerings of the highest kind, aiming toward
heaven and leading to supreme happiness. When he uses his wealth
properly, kings don't take it, thieves don't take it, fire doesn't take
it, floods don't take it, and unworthy heirs don't take it. His wealth,
used properly, goes to good ends, never to waste.*

—Samyutta Nikaya 3.19

THE BUDDHA HAD no problem with people making money,
or even becoming rich. Personal wealth is not a problem
unless it is not used well. The Buddha teaches rich people to be
responsible with their wealth by providing for family needs, employee needs, and the needs of friends. He also supports giving to
spiritual organizations in order to enrich the spiritual well-being
of everyone. In the quote, he emphasizes that good stewardship of
money guarantees that one's personal wealth will be secure from
threats and loss of all kinds.

This is naturally what a person of integrity does when wealthy.
But for many of us, integrity does not always come naturally, especially when we get rich. We are torn between our personal desires
and our commitment to live our values. Developing integrity is
like developing a muscle—the more you exercise it, the stronger
it gets. If our integrity is weak, we can act our way to right thinking. If we *act* as if we have integrity, in time we really will have it.

Creating a Long-Term Spending Plan

One quarter he spends on himself,
Two on his business,
The last he saves for times of need.
—Digha Nikaya 31

"PAY YOURSELF FIRST" is the advice of many wise financial planners. This means taking care of your personal well-being and expenses first. But employees and bosses alike get their financial priorities confused and end up in a pickle. Some become slaves to their creditors, paying their debts first and neglecting their own basic needs. Others pour every cent into their businesses, leaving themselves busy but broke. The Buddha famously rejected these extremes in life, and here we see him rejecting these extremes in finance. Why not follow the Buddha in applying a middle way? You don't have to divide your money exactly into quarters, but you should divide it into portions that are sensible, balanced, and far-sighted.

Here's a good question to ask yourself as you plan: "What plan will bring me peace?" We don't mean in the far future; we cannot be sure of that. We mean *now*. Your checking, credit, and savings accounts make the best fiscal Rorschach test. If you want to know what you really value and what your true priorities are, take a look at how you allocate your income: what you spend it on, how you invest it, and what you're willing to save for. Your accounts are the genuine bottom line here. Let them teach you who you are.

What percentage do you want to put into savings every month so that you have a cushion when hard times come (knowing that hard times *will* always come)? What percentage do you need to support yourself and your family in your needs and pleasures? What percentage do you want to give to help others? And what percentage do you want to plow back into your business or your career? Answer these questions honestly, and you will find a sense of financial peace.

Would the Buddha Caution Us about Greed?

Even heavenly pleasures don't distract
One who's pleased by ending of desire.
—Dhammapada 187

I T'S A GOOD thing the Buddha wasn't around for the "Me Decade" of the 1980s. He wouldn't have liked what he saw: conspicuous consumption, "looking out for number one," and "greed is good" were inescapable attitudes. "Tsk, tsk, tsk," the Buddha would have clucked. He would have seen through our mania for possessions to the restless vacancy that lies beneath the sparkling veneer of "have more, be happy."

Mother Teresa once remarked that the spiritual hunger she saw in the Western world was far worse that the physical hunger she saw in India. She, like the Buddha, knew that money and things can never make us happy—more things only make us want more things.

Real happiness comes when we become free of our cravings and stop the endless searching for something to satisfy them. When freed from our greed, we can again delight in pleasures. In fact, we can *truly* delight in pleasures for the first time, since until then, pleasure is veiled with the clinging film of desire.

What Should Mindful People Do If They Get Rich?

*That's how it is! Few are those who get rich and yet don't
become intoxicated and irresponsible from it, who don't get
greedy for sensual delight, who don't mistreat living things.*
—Samyutta Nikaya 3.6

THE PERSON WHO can get rich and not be ruined by it is rare.
Jesus said something like this as well: It is easier to fit a camel
(or perhaps a rope) through the eye of a needle than for a rich
person to get into heaven. Spiritual teachers work hard to keep us
from going astray. They see the seductive poison of money, and
they want to keep it from us. The Buddha himself grew up with
endless money and finally had to abandon it completely. He had
experienced firsthand how excessive money negatively affects us.

Money is a great temptation; it deludes us, it cajoles us, it
waits us out. It has implacable patience and terrible readiness. If
we have irresponsibility or greed in us, it will wait for its chance
and entice us to do the wrong thing.

So what would the Buddha do if he got rich? He showed us:
he turned away from a life of riches. If we don't have the freedom
to follow him financially, we must follow him internally. Our
minds must be free from the distortion of riches. We cannot be
greedy for the power and the sensual indulgence that they promote. We have to treat money like a visitor we respect but also
know is dangerous. We greet such a visitor cordially but do not
get too intimate, lest we be seduced. Living this way, we are free to
aid the world in material ways that the Buddha never could. Material and monetary giving is a vital part of right livelihood and
right action—that's a quarter of the eightfold path, right there.

How Would a Buddha Deal with Financial Setbacks and Losses?

View all problems as challenges. Look upon negativities that arise as opportunities to learn and to grow. Don't run from them, condemn yourself, or bury your burden in saintly silence. You have a problem? Great. More grist for the mill. Rejoice, dive in, and investigate.

—Bhante Henepola Gunaratana, *Mindfulness in Plain English*[1]

IT IS EASY to feel mindful, serene, and grateful when things are going well, especially financially. Many of us think that money is security, and for some of us, money is God. We revere money; we're convinced that if we only had more, all our problems would be solved. When we lose money, it feels like the end of the world. When we have no money, we feel we actually may die. So the real test of our character comes when times are tough, when we are facing adversity—especially financial adversity.

The Buddha understands our attachment to money and what it provides: an illusion of safety and fulfillment. He would empathize with, not condemn, our possessiveness, but he would not dwell with us there. He would coax us out the door of that burning house.

Among the smoking embers, the Buddha would give us a new frame for our broken financial situation. First, he would remind us that our value as human beings is not measured in dollars. We are not our money. So when we lose our money, we do not lose our value. Next, he would point out that humans learn best from their failures (indeed, some of us learn *only* from our failures). Third, he would teach that this applies to finance, just like anything else. Finally, he would remind us of all the wealthy, successful people throughout history who experienced bankruptcies, business failures, and personal disasters on their way to financial success. Who are we that we should think ourselves so different?

Many teachers have said that pain is the touchstone of all spiritual growth. Learn from your financial problems. Approach them with curiosity, not despair. And, as the Venerable Gunaratana says, do not add to your setbacks with ongoing blame. Look for the opportunity; look for the growth available in meeting your financial setbacks with a spirit of courage and openness.

How Would the Buddha Counsel People in Financial Hardship?

No matter how painful experience is,
if we lose our hope, that's our real disaster.
—The XIV Dalai Lama, on *Larry King Live*

THE DALAI LAMA has seen suffering: the loss of his entire nation. So how does he keep from losing hope? How does he keep smiling? He sees things as they are, not as they are *for him*. It is only when we see things as they really are that we can live integral lives, make integral actions and choices, and find integral happiness.

So, how *are* things, really? The Buddha taught *anicca* (impermanence). Impermanence comes, in turn, from *paticca-samuppada* ("dependent co-arising"), what contemporary Zen Master Thich Nhat Hanh calls, much more manageably, "interbeing." Later Buddhists evolved interbeing into *shunyata* ("emptiness" or, more accurately, "openness"). These are all views of the world that find the reality of things in their actual interactions, not in their doubtful essences. So the Buddha understood the dialectical nature of reality: that nothing is all good or all bad—that everything is both good *and* bad, and thus neither. What makes the difference is *us*. Our *experience* of the world makes our present, and what we *do* with the world determines our personal and collective future.

Some people respond to financial hardship by blaming others and portraying themselves as victims. There's a life's work there, a miserable one. Other people respond by seeing financial hardship as one more temporary situation to be transformed by taking initiative and getting into action that transforms those proverbial lemons into lucrative lemonade.

Many of the richest people on the planet experienced childhoods—even adulthoods—of extreme poverty, deprivation, and suffering. Oprah Winfrey, Sam Walton, and J. K. Rowling are just a few who have demonstrated that it doesn't matter where you come from—it only matters where you're going.

In every financial disaster you have a choice. You can give up and tell yourself, "It's hopeless." Or you can rise to the occasion, roll up your sleeves, and begin again.

How Should I Plan for My Retirement?

Do not chase after the past, nor pine for the future.
—Majjhima Nikaya 131

THE BUDDHA UNDERSTOOD the human mind. He noticed how much time we spend mulling over the past, replaying events again and again in our heads as if we were watching a favorite movie. He observed how often our imaginations fly into the future—planning, scheming, daydreaming, worrying, and wondering how our lives will turn out. Finally, the Buddha noted how little time we spend in the present, being awake to all that is unfolding around us and in us. In the *sutta* (the "scripture" that Majjhima Nikaya 131 denotes), he goes on to say, "What is present you clearly see right there, *right there*." Yet how much of our lives we miss, lost in the past or future.

It is in this present moment where we make choices that will determine so much of our lives to come. So the financial choices we make today contribute to our entire financial future. We make assumptions that the future is going to be more of what we have today, without realizing that our world can be turned upside down very quickly—as the global recession beginning in 2008 did with so many people's retirement goals. It is good to make plans, but it is not good to become attached to those plans. More often than not, plans are positions we can adapt as we gain more information and change perspective. And we don't mean just financially.

Our system encourages us to make retirement plans as if our lives are not going to change—ignoring the fact that our interests, needs, values, and preferences change fundamentally as we move into our later years. As we age, objects tend to lose their appeal, replaced by experiences, often inner ones. We may live lives of greater simplicity, but we may also live with expensive health challenges. Our financial needs may change dramatically, and we cannot predict when or how.

How would the Buddha plan his own retirement? He would focus on his work of the day. Part of that work would be taking advantage of the company retirement plan or setting up an IRA. Then it would be forgetting about that and getting back to doing good work.

🐚 Dealing with Change

*Riding the Waves of
Impermanence*

Why Do So Many People Resist Change, Even Change for the Good?

There is a wonderful little story about two monks who lived together in a monastery for many years; they were great friends. Then they died within a few months of one another. One of them got reborn in the heaven realms, the other monk got reborn as a worm in a dung pile. The one up in the heaven realms was having a wonderful time, enjoying all the heavenly pleasures. But he started thinking about his friend, "I wonder where my old mate has gone?" So he scanned all of the heaven realms, but could not find a trace of his friend. Then he scanned the realm of human beings, but he could not see any trace of his friend there, so he looked in the realm of animals and then of insects. Finally he found him, reborn as a worm in a dung pile . . . Wow! He thought: "I am going to help my friend. I am going to go down there to that dung pile and take him up to the heavenly realm so he too can enjoy the heavenly pleasures and bliss of living in these wonderful realms."

So he went down to the dung pile and called his mate. And the little worm wriggled out and said: "Who are you?" "I am your friend. We used to be monks together in a past life, and I have come up to take you to the heaven realms where life is wonderful and blissful." But the worm said: "Go away, get lost!" "But I am your friend, and I live in the heaven realms," and he described the heaven realms to him. But the worm said: "No thank you, I am quite happy here in my dung pile. Please go away." Then the heavenly being thought: "Well if I could only just grab hold of him and take him up to the heaven realms, he could see for himself." So he grabbed hold of the worm and started tugging at him; and the harder he tugged, the harder that worm clung to his pile of dung.

—Ajahn Brahm, *Who Ordered This Truckload of Dung?*[1]

W E FEAR CHANGE when we assume that change will be for the worse. We are more driven by fear of loss than by the promise of gain. Together, these traits produce our resistance to change. We feel that even if our current situation isn't perfect, it's familiar and predictable. And there's comfort in that.

But trouble comes when we resist opportunities due to this fear, when we resist despite good reasons to believe that change will be for the better. Well-meaning bosses or coworkers push us to accept change. They insist harder. We resist harder.

Understanding this about ourselves helps us to be compassionate with those who cling to the old and familiar while resisting the new and unknown. At one time or another, we have all been the worm, comfy in his warm, fragrant pile of shit, ignorant of what life has to offer, afraid to take a chance. As we forgive this in ourselves, we need to forgive it in others. Let your friends and coworkers be. They will change when they can. In the meantime, the best way to convince them that a change is good is to show how you yourself benefit when you let change happen. This adds new meaning to the well-known spiritual dictum: "Be the change you want to see in the world."

How Does a Buddha Face Anxiety, Fear, and Stress?

Everything together falls apart.
Everything rising up collapses.
Every meeting ends in parting.
Every life ends in death.
　　　　　　　—Udanavarga

WE'VE MENTIONED IMPERMANENCE as one of the core tenets of Buddhism. Everything falls apart. A corollary of impermanence is *anatta* (literally, "no-self"). All we value and care for, even our very self, is impermanent. We arise and we pass away, along with everything we love. There is no stopping this process. In the face of this, how do we feel?

Most of us feel anxiety, fear, and stress. Few of us can look directly into the face of change. The less control we have, the tighter we cling to the people, places, and things we are attached to. We worry about losing our jobs and money; our anxiety causes us to lose sleep, become irritable with our loved ones, and stress out over things we cannot now control, and later cannot stop.

Buddha knows. He once was where we are now. He saw the processes he described in the Udanavarga quote. He knew the worry, fear, anxiety, and stress that people experience. He knew that those processes are not what causes those feelings. He understood that it is our failure to understand the true nature of existence and impermanence that causes our pain and distress.

We want desperately to control the world around us, but the harder we try, the more upset we get as we refuse to accept that we can't control much of anything. We seek to find solid ground—in the form of secure jobs, money in the bank, loved ones who will never let us down or leave us, and so on. We are driven by fear as we search for something or someone to keep us safe and secure. But our efforts are futile. Sooner or later, we all discover that there is no place on the map called Safe. Contemporary Buddhist teacher Stephen Batchelor strongly warns against our attachment to place. We stand on a groundless ground. He is right: peace and serenity cannot be found and preserved any*place*: no job, no bank account, no family, no heart.

Peace lies in every moment; you must find it there. Your only job security is your ability to secure a job. Your emotional and spiritual well-being is a function of your relationship with yourself, including your ongoing dissolution. Ultimately, we *gain* neither happiness nor peace. When we really *accept* this, we open to the peace available to us in every moment.

How Should a Mindful Person Respond to Losing a Job?

That nothing is static or fixed, that all is fleeting and impermanent,
is the first mark of existence. It is the ordinary state of affairs.
Everything is in process. Everything—every tree, every blade of
grass, all the animals, insects, human beings, buildings, the animate
and the inanimate—is always changing, moment to moment.

—Pema Chödrön, *The Places That Scare You*[2]

EVERY BUDDHIST TEACHER, every *sutra*, every new Buddhist book, keeps relentlessly turning back to this central truth of *anicca*, impermanence. And it's as true at work as anywhere. There isn't a job on this planet that can't be—no, better, that *won't* be—outsourced, eliminated, changed, downsized, or abolished. Some are put on hold; others are gone for good. Some disappear to other countries; others vanish into thin air.

Of course, new jobs arise as old jobs vanish, but this may offer little consolation, as the new ones require different skills, knowledge, and aptitude than the old. For many of us, the world of work is a giant game of musical chairs: we go around and around until the music stops, we reach for the nearest chair, and it's been removed.

When you've lost your chair, here is what the Buddha says:

1. Don't take it personally. All jobs are impermanent. Your job is not "yours" or anybody's. It arose according to conditions that had nothing to do with you, and it passes away when conditions change.

2. Go sit down where the love is. Surround yourself with friends and family who will support and encourage you in this tough time. And do it for yourself. When Buddhists do *metta* practice, sending benevolence to the world, they begin with themselves.

3. Draw on spiritual resources to get you through the pain of losing a job. Meditate, pray, read inspirational literature,

find spiritual teachers, join a spiritual community, spend time in nature, listen to or play music, journal about your feelings. Teachers and traditions have been laying up these treasures for you for four thousand years. You have free time now; this is your chance to dig in!

4. Remember, just as jobs pass away, so does joblessness. Impermanence can also be your friend. Along with that old job, let go of your job assumptions, your job limitations, your job preconditions. Make those impermanent, too. Now you're open, ready to respond when the music plays again.

Does the Buddha Have Any Wisdom about Changing Careers?

"Nothing really dies," I told him. "It just turns into something else. Everything is always changing form. Do you remember the pumpkin that rotted into the earth in your garden? Tomatoes sprouted where it used to be. This bird will go back to the earth and turn into lavender flowers and butterflies."

—Anne Cushman, "What Is Death, Mommy?" in *The Best Buddhist Writing 2006*[3]

THE BUDDHA CHANGED career in major ways three times before hitting on something that stuck. And those changes were seriously downwardly mobile. In his first career, he was heir apparent to the family business: running a fiefdom of the Kosalan kingdom. Sweet set-up. And the myths make it sweeter: protected from all *dukkha* in his various palaces and gardens, the best at everything he tried. He was one of those wonder boys who bosses go gaga for; he couldn't do wrong.

But even for the golden boy, it fell apart. Like most golden boys, he eventually discovered that his little world just didn't match reality. In the myth, Siddhartha (he wasn't the Buddha yet) sees a sick person, an old person, a dead person, and an ascetic; in our lives, we see dysfunctional groups, people playing out the string until they're vested, people in tedious or dead-end jobs, and people quitting.

So he made his first career change: he walked out on his job, giving up the promise of becoming CEO. He became a *bhikkhu*, the Pali word for "monk." But literally it means "beggar." That, friends, is the courage to begin at the very bottom. He sought out spiritual mentors and teachers to show him the way to spiritual awakening. Unfortunately, they couldn't do it. They showed him austerities, meditations, self-mortifications, and he excelled in them. He even attracted a little crowd of five disciples, who followed him around thinking he was the best, which he was. But what was the use? He was a glorious success in his second career by any standard but his own: he was the best faster, the best meditator, but he could not solve the question of why we suffer. So he quit. Again.

He ate a little rice dish that a peasant offered him, and his disciples turned away. For them—for the crowd—he had abandoned the correct way. For himself, he was beginning his third career: independent seeker. And once he found this new path, this middle way, he quickly found the answers to his questions. He sat under the Bodhi tree and meditated, determined to go within and find the answers he had failed to find in external circumstances. He began to teach, and he never stopped until his final breath.

Along the way, Siddhartha did the things that any smart career changer would do:

1. Drop a career that makes you miserable. Life is short. Move on and try something new, and keep trying new things until you find what works for you.

2. Listen to the advice of people who love you (like your parents) and to experts (like spiritual teachers), but do not obey them blindly. Test what they say against your own

intuitive heart in deciding which path is right for you. Think for yourself, as Siddhartha did.

3. Take time to know yourself. Learn what makes you tick. Discover what makes you truly happy, not superficially but deeply. It takes time and focused attention to learn this. Do not skimp. Ask hard questions of yourself.

4. Once you know what you want, take action. Do not linger in situations that make you unhappy, just for the sake of your family's wishes or for money. Don't sell your soul for a paycheck or for others' approval. Walk your own path. Do you think it was easy for Siddhartha to walk away from his first career into the absolute unknown, giving away everything he ever knew? But he was the *Buddha*, you say? Not yet. He was just like us—an unhappy guy who knew that life should be more.

How Can You Go about Finding New, Mindful Work?

It's never too late. Even if you are going to die tomorrow, keep yourself straight and clear and be a happy human being today. If you keep your situation happy day by day, you will eventually reach the greatest happiness of enlightenment.
—Lama Thubten Yeshe, *The Bliss of Inner Fire*[4]

THE BUDDHA WAS a practical teacher. He didn't espouse pie-in-the-sky, feel-good, woo-woo stuff. Right livelihood is part of the eightfold path. Let's see how he might coach you in finding that livelihood.

1. Stay connected to your network of colleagues, friends, and family. Interdependence is as central to the Buddha's teachings as impermanence. Even monks are meant to live

in community, in relationships, in partnerships, in connection to other people. You interact with these folks; let them know your situation.

2. Search for *work*, not for "a job." The nature of work has been changing for many years now, with a shift from full-time, 9-to-5 positions to project work, or portfolio work, in which people are hired to work on a project and then move on when the project is done. People in construction and in the entertainment industry have worked like this for years. There is still plenty of work to be done; it's just, well, impermanent.

3. Don't look for security—look for *opportunity*. Security and safety are illusions, fabricated in our minds' longing to stand on solid ground. There is none. Life is risky and dangerous—breathe . . . feel your fear . . . now get out and live anyway.

4. Look for opportunities to serve others. Offer to help people in whatever ways you can. Invest in the interpersonal bank. You must make deposits in the bank before you can make withdrawals—and this is as true with the interpersonal bank as it is with the financial bank. When are you going to do this investing? When you're busy with new work? Invest your time *now*.

5. Consider doing volunteer work. It's easy to slip into self-pity and depression when you're looking for work. As we advised in another answer, when you're discouraged, encourage others. It's amazing how this works. Having commitments to help others keeps you off the pity-pot and involved with the world. And sometimes, volunteer work leads to paid work—you never can tell. You only know you are being a bodhisattva. That's good already. And since you might believe in that little thing called karma, need we say more?

How Can You Take Good Care of Yourself in Difficult Times?

> *By knowing yourself, you're coming to know humanness altogether.*
> *. . . Then you'll be changing old stuck patterns that are shared by*
> *the whole human race. Compassion for others begins with kindness*
> *to ourselves.* —Pema Chödrön, *Start Where You Are*[5]

GOOD SELF-CARE IS important all the time, but especially in times of change, stress, confusion, loss, and pain. You can't heal the world until you make yourself at least ambulatory.

Begin with the basics: get plenty of sleep, drink your water, eat healthy foods, and get some exercise, even if it's just walking around the block. Basic self-care takes neither a lot of time nor a lot of money—but it does take seeing yourself as worth it. You are.

In tough times, it's tempting to comfort ourselves with junk food and other junk pleasures. We turn to alcohol, sweets, TV, shopping: quick ways to turn off mindfulness of our pain. But like a firm mother, the Buddha would guide us (gently, sure, always gently, but still firmly) away from these distractions. As a mother would care for her only child, so should we care for ourselves. Yes, a chocolate or a trashy TV show to soothe the senses when we're sick, but then time for a little healthy soup and a good book.

Seeking comfort is natural and normal in times of distress and pain, but ultimately the only way out of the pain is *through* it. The greatest kindness to ourselves is to heal ourselves. After all, there are so many others who need our care!

PART II

🦠 Cultivating Mindful Work Relationships

*When awakened by all things, the separateness of you
and others drops away.* —Dogen Zenji, Genjo Koan

"HELL IS OTHER PEOPLE," wrote the French philosopher Jean-Paul Sartre. He was half right. The other half is "Heaven is other people, too." To work in an organization necessarily means working with other people—coworkers, bosses, customers, vendors, the public. Our relationships with other people are what give us most of our headaches—but these relationships can also give us much joy.

Bankers have been heard to mutter, "This would be a great place to work, if it weren't for the customers." University staff people sometimes comment, "This would be a great place to work, if it weren't for the students." Book publishers (not *ours*, of course, never *never*) occasionally gripe, "This would be a great place to work, if it weren't for the authors." Wherever you work, we are sure that you too can identify groups of people that make your life difficult. Bosses complain about their workers; workers complain about their bosses.

Isn't it funny how everyone seems to think that someone *else* is the problem? And yet, many people who work from home complain that the thing they miss the most is other people!

What are we to do? We can't seem to live with one another, but we can't live without one another. Woody Allen summarized our predicament nicely at the end of his movie *Annie Hall*, when he turned to the camera to comment on an old joke.

This guy goes to a psychiatrist and says, "Doc, my brother's crazy— he thinks he's a chicken." And the doctor says, "Well, why don't you turn him in?" And the guy says, "I would, but I need the eggs." Well, I guess that's pretty much how I feel about relationships. You know, they're totally irrational and crazy and absurd and . . . but I guess we keep going through it . . . because . . . most of us need the eggs.

The Buddha understood this dilemma, and much of his teaching addresses how to live in community with other people. How we can work together in organizations, getting the "eggs" we all need and not hurting each other in the process. The following pages will help you accomplish this difficult goal, without having to walk on eggshells.

The Buddha teaches that we truly exist only in our relationships. This is why their power is so great. This is why they can be heaven or hell for us. Relationships are eternal; we are not. Whether picking leaders or building teams or training employees or ending conflicts, we are creating relationships; we are working through relationships. The Buddha's teaching can make those relationships the path of awakening itself.

❀ Working with Others

Unity in Diversity

How Does Mindfulness Help Us to Get Along with Others?

He gives what is dear, does what is hard, bears what is painful,
admits his secrets, keeps others', helps those in need, and never
rejects the ruined.   —Anguttara Nikaya 7.35

THE PATH TO mindful work is definitely not the easier, softer way. The Buddha knows that in order to move beyond suffering and find happiness, we must give up many of the things that at first seem most natural for us. As humans, it is our inclination to look for the easy way to do things, to hold on to things we treasure, to avoid pain, to hide our secrets from others, to gossip about others' secrets, and to avoid people who are of a lower status or those who have been ruined by some life circumstance. However, if we follow these inclinations, we will not cultivate good relationships with others at work. It really *will* be a "looking out for number one" kind of workplace, and everyone will be miserable.

If I want good relationships with my coworkers, I should follow the Buddha's coaching as best I can: give to others even when I feel selfish; take on hard jobs that need doing; put up with difficult things without complaining; be honest, admit my mistakes, and ask for help; keep confidences that others share with me; help coworkers in need; and be loyal to friends who may be going through scandal or disgrace. If I want these things from others, then I must start by *giving* them first.

What Would the Buddha Say about the Golden Rule?

Philip asked Suzuki why the Japanese make their teacups so thin and delicate that they break easily. "It's not that they're too delicate, but that you don't know how to handle them. You must adjust yourself to the environment, and not vice versa."
—David Chadwick, *To Shine One Corner of the World*[1]

THE BUDDHA UNDERSTOOD the ego and our tendency to use ourselves as the yardstick by which to evaluate and judge everything and everyone. Our ego is a handy yardstick, but an inaccurate one as well, because anything different is likely to seem defective.

The intention behind the golden rule is good: treating others the way we want to be treated generally makes for good relationships. But there's a significant flaw in this thinking: it assumes that everyone is like you. Look even at your family and you see this is not the case. Human beings are surely as different as snowflakes. They may appear to be the same at first glance, but when we look closer, we discover striking differences.

The Buddha might suggest exchanging the golden rule for the triple gem. Treat others the way *they* want to be treated. Rather than criticizing the teacup for being "too fragile," consider changing the way *you* hold the teacup. Instead of judging other people to be "different" (and therefore difficult), consider finding out more about them so that your relationship is truly mutual. In a global marketplace with a pluralistic workforce, flexibility and adaptability are not optional; they are fundamental practices.

In fact, there is a Buddhist version of the golden rule: "Do not harm others in ways in which you wish not to be harmed" (Udanavarga 5.18 [139]). What we want varies wildly, but what we want to avoid is much the same all over. So, be more modest in exporting your egoism, and adjust yourself to the environment.

Will Being Buddha at Work Enable Me to Influence Others?

He possesses wonderful eloquence for deep truths. He is
extremely skilled in explaining positions and reconciling opposites.
His eloquence is unstoppable; his sure intellect irresistible.
—Vimalakirtinirdesha Sutra 5

THINK OF SOMEONE you know at work who is very influential—someone whom others listen to and respect. What makes that person influential? Unless the person happens to be in the boss's family, she's influential for two reasons: competence and character.

We respect someone because she is competent, skillful in her work; she is talented, smart, and well trained, and she achieves results. We also respect her because she has good character: she is honest, compassionate, hardworking, responsible, and ethical; she takes initiative; and she is a good person.

To be influential, you must have both competence and character. You must know your own job and do it well; and you must be seen to have integrity—to consistently do well and do what you say. To tie it all together, if you can develop the ability to be consistently articulate, there will be absolutely no stopping you in your career! Your influence will be irresistible.

If you're not as articulate as you'd like to be, perhaps now's the time to sign up for Toastmasters (or in this case, perhaps Taoistmasters).

Is It Important to "Go the Extra Mile" for Others?

*Giving is the highest expression of the goodwill of the
powerful. Even dust, if given in naive ignorance, is a good gift.
Because its effect is so great, no gift given in good faith to a
worthy recipient is small.* —Jatakamala 3.23

THE BUDDHA TAUGHT, on a profound level, what we've all
heard for years: "It's the thought that counts." Mind matters.
A generous mind always finds something to give.

Smart bosses know that appreciation is what motivates people. The gift of a smile, or a few well-spoken words of praise in public, or a small token of recognition can go a long way to making folks feel cared for and acknowledged. More-substantial gifts can also be very effective when given in good faith. But be careful; small gifts and trinkets often backfire when they seem condescending, superficial, or manipulative. Gifts must be meaningful to the recipient if they are to be effective. Otherwise, employees see right through them and become cynical.

Smart employees know that they too have the power of giving. Doing a little something extra for the customer engenders loyalty and generates repeat and referral business. Doing something extra for a coworker is a way of investing in the interpersonal bank, so that when you need help, you have goodwill to draw on. Gifts of attention, concern, and interest are powerful ways to build relationships with one another, and going the extra mile builds trust, teamwork, and strong morale.

There are thousands of ways to do a little something extra for others:

- Bring in flowers from your home garden and give them to someone.

- Ask what you can do to help if a coworker seems stressed or frantic.

- Give your boss an article that you think would interest him.
- Throw in a little something extra when a customer makes a big purchase.
- Throw in a little something extra when a customer has a problem.
- Offer to stay late to help meet an important deadline.
- Ask about coworkers' families—show that you care about them as people.
- Get involved in company-sponsored activities and programs, like Junior Achievement, United Way, blood drives, local Boys and Girls clubs, and so on.

Doing something extra is always good, not only for the other person but for you as well. These are esteem-able acts.

How Can We Mindfully Address the Double Standard That We Often Hold between Ourselves and Others?

Others' faults and errors are so plain,
But our own are difficult to see.
—Dhammapada 252

HAVE YOU EVER noticed the double standard we use when we're evaluating someone else's behavior versus our own? Oh yeah, you've noticed it when others employ it! But here is why you don't see it in yourself: we judge ourselves by our *intentions*, while we judge others by their *behavior*. Not fair! And the Buddha warns us against it, just as Jesus did (see Matthew 7:3). We "make mistakes"; others "commit errors."

Think about it. This is why we're so quick to judge other people's faults and errors: it's so easy to see them. We give them no credit at all for good intentions, because we cannot read their minds. But when it comes to our own behavior, we know we meant well and we reward ourselves for it. "That wasn't my intention; I didn't *mean* for that to happen." We try to clothe our mistakes with purity of purpose, and we expect others to understand and forgive us.

Yet again, this arises from the delusion that people are separate from one another, when in actuality we are all connected and interrelated. If we ever reach the day when we *get it* that we're not separate, this double standard will disappear. Until that day, the Buddha suggests we give others the benefit of the doubt. As you give yourself credit, give it to others.

Is It Okay to Have a "Work Spouse"?

Tanzan and Ekido were walking down a muddy road in the rain. As they came around a bend, they saw a lovely woman in a silk kimono and sash, unable to cross the mud.

"Come on," said Tanzan, and carried her over.

Ekido did not speak until that night. When he couldn't remain silent any longer, he asked, "We monks do not touch women, especially beautiful ones. It's forbidden. Why did you carry her?"

Tanzan replied, "I set her down at the corner; are you still carrying her?" —The Book of Sand and Stones, case 14

WHEN MEN AND WOMEN spend long hours working together, sometimes close friendships develop, as pairs of people find themselves united by common interests, similar duties and responsibilities, and even shared suffering in a competitive corporate climate or in dealing with the same difficult boss. It is understandable if these pairs develop a camaraderie that goes beyond the typical coworker status. But is it good?

The story gives us the answer: what matters is what's happening inside your head. You can be Ekido and follow the rules and be filled with *dukkha*. But you can also be Tanzan, disregard the rules, and be free from dukkha. There is nothing inherently good or bad about touching a woman. There is nothing inherently good or bad about having a work spouse as well as a home spouse. The rightness of these actions depends on our intentions and interactions. If you're able to have a special friendship with a coworker without its threatening or detracting from your love and commitment to your home spouse, no problem.

Does Being Mindful Make You a Better Listener?

The unlistening one grows like a bull.
His muscles swell, but not his brain or wisdom.
—*Dhammapada 152*

"GOD GAVE US two ears and only one mouth; we should use them in that proportion." Many successful leaders repeat this, and their success testifies to the truth of the saying.

The single most underdeveloped and underutilized skill in organizations of all types and all sizes is the skill of listening. It is amazing how much you can learn, how smart you can become, simply by *listening*. The Buddha tells us that we don't become wise by talking; we become wise by listening. Do you think the Buddha spent the years leading to his enlightenment talking or listening?

Listening individually, you learn from others. Listening in groups, when the whole group listens attentively, we learn even more. For example, in Native American–based council practices (where participants commit to always listening as others speak and thus cannot pre-think their own words), we learn about others, we learn about ourselves, and we learn who we are together as a group. Real listening frees you to learn in these new ways.

How Does a Buddha Receive Negative Feedback?

When I receive productive words, unsought,
That counsel me in useful, skillful ways,
I should gratefully accept them, always
Looking out to learn from everyone.
—Bodhicharyavatara 5.74

I F THERE IS one thing most of us hate, it is unsolicited advice or criticism. It hurts our feelings; we're not prepared to hear it. We didn't ask for anyone's feedback, and we bristle with resentment. Rooted in this negative mind-set, anger bubbles up. All this makes it so hard to learn from unasked-for counsel.

The compassionate scholar and monk Shantideva here urges you to let go of your ego and recognize the value of listening to other people's feedback, perhaps *especially* when you didn't ask for it. If you give in to resentment, you learn from no one. If you are grateful, you learn from everyone. If you truly want to be wise, you will view everyone as your teacher. The most important lessons you need to learn may come from very unlikely sources. Listen carefully when someone gives you an admonition: it may be the Buddha talking to you.

The Trick to Training Coworkers

I shouldn't show the road with just a finger,
But instead, using a respectful
Gesture, stretching out my proper arm,
I should indicate the path ahead.
—Bodhicharyavatara 5.94

THE MOST IMPORTANT thing to keep in mind when training or teaching someone else is respect. Above all, you must respect the learner and honor the fact that she is where she is on her own career and spiritual path. If you would teach her, you must meet her where she is. Then you can invite her to travel further down the path by learning what you are offering to teach. Do not tell her what to do—rather, invite her to do what you are suggesting and embodying. When you project genuine energy in sharing your knowledge, your learners will want to learn with you.

Well, usually. Every learner has the power to agree or to refuse to learn. The teacher cannot control this. Both BJ and Franz have plenty of experience with noncooperative learners. When we're wise, we recognize and honor our learners' choices—even the choices to be late, to be rude, to not show up, and so on. If you want to help others travel the road of mindful work, *invite* them—don't *tell* them. This path is sometimes hard. When you show, in your teaching, your own commitment to learning, you honor both the learner and the process. If the learner doesn't respond, you have your own teaching job to do. Be impeccable and you'll still find satisfaction in the work.

How Can We Give Negative Feedback in a Constructive Manner?

In criticizing, the teacher is hoping to teach. That's all.
—Zen Teacher Bankei, Dialogues

B ANKEI HAD TRAINED for years to cultivate his Buddha mind, and he was of course a teacher himself. He knew both how hard it is to change and how hard it is to help another to change. He knew that in this process there are times when criticism is necessary, and here he tells how to give it. His teaching is so simple, but so powerful.

When criticizing another, the teacher always hopes to teach. That's it. The teacher never criticizes to make a point, to show off his wit, or to establish his own superiority. He criticizes only to teach. If you cannot maintain the mind of teaching when criticizing, you should not criticize.

When you get an impulse to criticize, ask yourself, "Am I about to teach something? Am I free of all motives other than teaching?" You could be teaching the person you are criticizing, or someone else who needs to learn, and you should always be teaching yourself, learning from your actions. But unless your answer is an honest and immediate "Yes, the critique is simply to teach," hold your tongue.

Of course, this whole discussion implies that the person on the receiving end of your criticism is open and receptive to it. Do not overlook this. Do not assume that everyone is interested in learning from your insight and comments. Do not just assume the role of teacher with everyone you know, let alone the role of critic. This is especially true of your coworkers and bosses. If you are a supervisor or manager, it is your job to criticize your employees if that will help them improve. But with everyone else, it is a good idea to ask them first: "I have some observations that might help you. Would you like some feedback?" If they say yes, you can criticize them and help them learn. If they say no, forget it.

Does Being Buddha at Work Encourage Personal Accountability in Others?

Don't look at others' wrongs, done or undone.
See what you, yourself, have done or not.
—Dhammapada 50

ONE TEACHING THE Buddha constantly returned to was that we're responsible for our own lives. In every situation, we can choose to play the role of victim and blame others, or we can own the problem and thereby take responsibility for the solution.

The Buddha is wise to emphasize how we're powerless to change other people. In fact, we can change *ourselves* only with concentrated effort. It does no good to focus on others' shortcomings and faults when we aren't in a position to do anything about them. Let's not be distracted; for most of us, there is plenty of work to be done in respect to ourselves.

Best to sweep our own side of the street and let others deal with theirs. Being personally accountable yourself is the best way to set an example and encourage others to follow suit. That's what the Buddha did. He lived his life in full accountability, and eventually he was *completely surrounded by others who wanted to live the same way.*

If you live a life of personal accountability and others like the results you're getting, they will emulate you and become personally accountable as well. You will influence others through a process of attraction and osmosis, not scolding and evangelizing.

How Can You Help Friends and Loved Ones to Deal with Unwanted Change?

Mindfulness must be engaged. Once there is seeing, there must be acting. Otherwise, what is the use of seeing?

We must be aware of the real problems of the world. Then, with mindfulness, we know what to do and what not to do to be of help.

—Thich Nhat Hanh, *Peace Is Every Step*[2]

U NDERSTANDING THE PROCESS of change is enormously helpful to people going through it. If we know that there are five predictable stages to our emotional/psychological response to change, we are better able to tolerate our pain—knowing that it won't last forever.

When a significant change happens in our life, the first stage of our reaction process is *shock* that often segues into denial. "This can't be happening," we think to ourselves. Or "This couldn't happen to me."

As the shock wears off and we come out of denial, the next stage is *anger, frustration, resentment.* "How could they let this happen?" we complain to one another. "This isn't fair!" we lament. "I hate this!" we tell anyone still willing to listen.

As we vent our rage and sense of betrayal, our turmoil runs its course and we enter the third stage of change—*resignation.* Here we at last hit emotional bottom. We feel spent, left with only a melancholy acceptance and perhaps depression. Resistance is futile; the bemoaned change is a fait accompli, and there's just nothing we can do about it.

But the mind can't stay still for long. We begin to move into the fourth stage of change: *exploration and experimentation.* "Well, maybe I'll give that a try," we think to ourselves. Or "I wonder if I could make this work." Or perhaps, "Hmmm, this might not be as awful as I thought." With our baby steps forward, we look up. We imagine light at the end of the tunnel. As our vision brightens, so do our visions.

We experiment with tentative steps into the new reality with which we are faced. It's like walking out of Plato's cave. Scary. We try a few things—some work, some don't. But we keep going until we arrive at the final stage of change: *revitalization*. We adjust to what has happened and commit to a new future. Life—we realize, by the way—is good.

These five stages of change are the same for everyone, but each individual moves through them at his or her own pace. To help others through this process, we need to honor them as they progress through these predictable stages of change.

What can we do to help? We begin with compassion: we let ourselves feel their pain. This is fundamental. When another is in pain, we move first to soothe them. We witness and validate their feelings. Then we put our compassion in the context of wisdom. We tell them they are not crazy—their emotions are normal and right, and they can look forward to the process we described above.

On the basis of mindfulness, we know how to help. Through our own work, we are prepared to help others do their own. We can do much to help our coworkers, friends, and family with the process of change. We are all wounded healers, and in sharing our own journey through the pain of change, we can help others on their journey.

Dealing with Difficult People

Seeing All Beings as the Buddha

How Do Mindful People Deal with Jerks?

As a result of our own lies and gossip we face bad workers and mean people. Whether it's our students, our helpers, or our employees, they argue with us. They disagree without even paying attention to us. They pretend not to understand until we repeat things two or three times; then they get angry with our tone and talk back and take their own sweet time to do the work. When they finally finish, they don't get around to telling us, and they continue to be spiteful and angry.

—Dzogchen Kunzan Lama 83

HOW DOES THIS horrible situation happen to us? Why is the world so unfair?

The Buddha's answer turns the tables on you. You want to know the reason why everyone is treating you so badly? It's because you started it long before. Everyone knows the saying "What goes around comes around." It doesn't apply just to others; it applies to *you*. It was your own hostility, your own duplicity, that began the cycle that led to your current situation. (We know . . . this isn't the answer you wanted to hear.)

Perhaps you don't even remember how it began. Perhaps you think you never treated these people badly. Perhaps you are even right about that. But can you honestly say that you've never lied in a work situation? Can you claim that you have never gossiped about someone and said things that were hurtful? We didn't think so. There are no innocents among us. People are jerks to us because at some time or other we have been jerks to others. Other people are mirrors of ourselves.

Okay, so the Buddha tells you why you're faced with these bad relationships. Now what to do about them? It is very simple and also very difficult. You began this cycle of negativity; you are going to have to end it. When you face anger, show compassion. When you encounter inattention, attend to what those people are really thinking. When you wait through delays, maintain mindfulness of your reactions to those annoyances. When you receive no thanks, remember your reward is precisely in that lesson.

Not so easy. Yes, we're with you. But it's not forever, and by staying mindful, you may dramatically change your future path. Dealing with a jerk may be perfect preparation for the next steps in your career—we never know whether and how something painful might turn out to be a blessing later. Don't give in to your anger or that of others; just keep your mouth shut and, without even knowing why, take responsibility. That is the bodhisattva path.

How Should You Deal with Coworkers Who Lie?

Animals express their true feelings in their cries.
Only humans are smart enough to hide the truth.
—Jatakamala 22.19

THE HUMAN CAPACITY for self-awareness is both our blessing and our curse. We feel, and yet we have the capacity to stand outside ourselves, to feel ourselves feeling something, and to choose whether or not to let others know. In other words, we always have the choice to express our thoughts and feelings or to express something different.

This ability to dissemble causes a lot of trouble at work. People lie at work when they feel they must hide the truth. They may think that if they disagree with the boss, it will hurt their career. If they point out the weakness in a business idea, they'll be branded as "not a team player." Such beliefs teach us to lie. We end up with whole organizations full of people lying to one another. Hard to be mindful and awake if you have to lie about what you see and think.

The Buddha would be compassionate about all this lying. He knows that coworkers who lie are not bad people; they have just lived in an environment of lying for so long that they're blind to how much it harms them. People often have blind spots that prevent them from seeing how self-destructive their own actions are.

The Buddha would encourage leaders to transform their organizations by rewarding people for telling the truth, no matter how bitter, and by not rewarding lies, no matter how sweet. He would tell workers not to sell their integrity for a paycheck. No paycheck is worth that price. The Buddha would invite all of us to emulate the clarity of animals—to say what we mean and mean what we say.

How Do You Handle People Pleasers?

A sycophant is an enemy pretending to be a friend in four phases: he agrees with whatever you did in the past; he agrees with all your plans for the future; he makes empty promises to gain favor; then— when he can actually do something—he says he just can't.

—Digha Nikaya 31

OST OF US have met charmers like this at work. They are so eager to curry favor, they are so desperate to be liked, that they will flatter you, agree with you, say just about anything to please you. After enough time, you realize that, unfortunately, you can't believe a thing they say—neither about what you've done nor about what they will do for you.

This is a crucial lesson, because you cannot have your own work, or your team's, undermined by the false expectations that sycophants create. If others tell you only what they think you want to hear, you're not getting the whole story, and their misinformation can easily trip you up. Do not base your decisions or actions on the input from people pleasers.

This is especially true for business owners, executives, and managers. A smart boss in a healthy organization trains his followers to tell him the truth, no matter what. An emotionally mature leader makes it safe for his staff to disagree with him, to express alternative points of view, even to argue with him, if they feel strongly that their boss is mistaken.

Your real friend is the one who gives you authentic, accurate feedback—both positive and negative. She is your teacher, and your entire organization should be grateful to her. And when it comes to yourself, emulate her, not the sycophant.

How Should You Respond If Someone Bad-Mouths You?

A bad person who slanders a good one is like a person who looks up and spits at heaven. His spit never reaches the sky; it falls back into his own face. —Sutra of Forty-two Sections 8

WHEN SOMEONE IS trashing you, it is often hard to remember that in the long run, this is going to come back and hurt the person doing the trashing. The Buddha helps you to keep the proper perspective. Perhaps you wish the trash talker would get his comeuppance as fast as the person who spits at heaven. Stop wasting your time with these thoughts.

The Buddha's simile tells us another crucial thing about this situation. When you are bad-mouthed, you are like heaven in the simile. Does heaven spit back at the bad-mouther? No. It is the bad-mouther's own bile that comes back at him. It is the same when someone bad-mouths you. Do not respond in kind. Do not sink to that level. Let gravity simply take its course and the bad words find their way home. No effort is required; this is just the way of things.

The Buddha is in a good position to know this—he was constantly getting slandered by jealous religious figures. He just let it be. Things turned out pretty well for him, didn't they? (And, hey, you don't have to rise to the celestial purity of the Buddha; you just have to stay out of spitting range.)

How Do Buddhas Deal with Anger?

"He insulted me, he beat me, robbed me!"
Think this way and hatred never ends.
"He insulted me, he beat me, robbed me!"
Give this up and in you hatred ends.
Not by hate is hate defeated; hate is
Quenched by love. This is eternal law.

                                        —Dhammapada 3–5

CONFLICT IS A fact of organizational life. Following their desires and attachments, people are bound to hurt one another in the course of working together. But conflict's naturalness doesn't mean that we should let it continue.

So how should we handle workplace hurts and conflicts? We naturally want to respond in kind when others are hostile toward us, but the Buddha tells us to resist this inclination. Other people's hostility often has nothing to do with us—they are just acting out their own karma. If we meet others' anger with our own anger, joining in their negative karma, we are simply adding fuel to the fire, endangering everyone, including ourselves.

Instead, the Buddha counsels us to take the high road—to respond to others' hostility with compassion and forgiveness. Wise teachers throughout the ages have echoed the Buddha's wisdom: Jesus, Gandhi, Martin Luther King Jr., and so many others in other cultures. The soothing balm of unconditional love and understanding is the only thing that calms hostility in others.

Is this a tall order? Of course it is. We are human, after all, and the Buddha knows this. But harboring a resentment because someone else hurt us is like swallowing poison and hoping the other person will die. And acting vengefully, taking an eye for an eye, only leads us to the kingdom of the blind. We must forgive and let go of revenge—otherwise we become prisoners of our own anger. Quench your hate in the waters of love. It's a slow business, but a sweet one.

What Would the Buddha Caution about Adulterous Affairs at Work?

Four things for one who beds another's wife:
Loss, unrest, censure, and finally hell.

—Dhammapada 309

THE BUDDHA WOULD say the same thing about sexual affairs whether they happen at work or someplace else: adulterous affairs are costly to the illicit lovers. The text above outlines what will happen to the male partner; we can assume that the female partner will pay a similar price. Note that we're not talking about single people, free to find intimacy where they can. We are talking about adultery here.

First, the lovers will immediately feel degraded and will lose the respect of those who know about the affair. Second, the lovers will lose sleep because of their guilty consciences and their worry about being found out by their spouses and everyone else. Third, the lovers may very well be censured. It is not uncommon that one partner or the other may be forced to resign if the affair becomes a matter of public knowledge and the boss (or the human resources department) finds out about it. Adulterous affairs are costly to an organization in terms of gossip, morale, attention, and productivity, and smart managers and executives act quickly to discipline the illicit lovers.

Finally, the lovers will pay the price of hell. Not necessarily hell of the fire and brimstone kind, ruled by the red guy with tail and horns, but the hell of being trapped by desire, attachment, deception, lying, broken vows, and more. Hell is where we live when we spite the path of awakening and choose instead to be slaves to our desires.

The Buddha would mince no words in counseling adulterers about the cost of their extramarital affair. His own censure would be compassionate, but there's not much he'd be able to do to save these lovers from the results of their own actions.

How Should I Respond to Whiners and Negative People?

Don't stay with friends who cheat or do what's base.
Stay with noble friends; stay with the best.

—Dhammapada 78

THE BUDDHA DOESN'T mince words with his advice: avoid whiners, chronic complainers, and any other negative people. Avoid them like the plague. Why? Because it's contagious. Just as a drunk wants you drunk, too, if you're going to be around him, so whiners want you to join in their whining. It's easy to get sucked into the negative energy of negative people—we all have frustrations and complaints about work, and sometimes it even seems like fun to join in the pile-on of cynicism and anger. But don't do it. Resist the pack mentality that transforms these negative people into jackals. Run away if you must.

Instead, seek out positive people at work. Look for people who are up to something good and hang out with them. Make a list of the five or ten most admired people where you work and see if you can find ways to spend some time with them. Remember: they too want to spend time with sincere people; that means you. At the very least, watch them from a distance and see what you can learn from them.

Associate with honest people, good people, people who are good at their jobs. If you want a good future, hang out with the best. Why? Because that's contagious, too.

What Should I Do If I Have a Conflict with a Teammate?

When conflict arises in your own family, don't blame others.
Instead, look for the cause in your own mind and action and
pursue the solution there. —Anguttara Nikaya 3.31

PEACE WITHIN A team, like peace within a family, is vital to the well-being of both individuals and the group. Blaming someone else does no good at all—in fact, it makes things worse. If you think the problem lies in someone else, then the solution must lie there as well. There's nothing you can do; you're powerless. This is no way to be. Instead, if *you* own the problem, then you begin to own the solution. You will think of what you can do to make things better (no matter what the other person is doing).

When team conflict arises, ask yourself, "How have I contributed to this situation?" You know it takes two to tango; it's doubtful that you are ever simply an innocent victim. (And if somehow you *are* an innocent victim, drop that role now. Own the problem and empower yourself to end it.) Look for what you can do to contribute to a solution. Victims assign blame; winners make things better. In the end, would you rather be the one who's morally right or the one who's fixed the problem? (Hint: which one do you think your company prefers?)

❀ Customers—
Love 'Em or Lose 'Em

Customer Service as
Bodhisattva Activity

What Does the Buddha Tell Us about Serving Customers?

May I be, in many ways, a support for all the living beings
throughout space, for as long as all are not yet satisfied!
—Bodhicharyavatara 3.22

THE BUDDHA TAUGHT that serving others is our true work, no matter what kind of job we may happen to have. For it is through serving others that we overcome our own natural self-centeredness. This is the true work of the whole world, for in this work we all escape *dukkha* together. As long as we are focused on ourselves, we continue to feel the pull of desires and attachments; but when we turn our attention to the needs of others, we find happiness, and we're freed from our own endless wanting.

Today the Buddha would tell us that customer service people are the most important people in our organization. If the organization exists to serve the needs of clients or customers (and why else would an organization exist?), its most important members must be those who most directly serve them. This remains true whether you work for a money-making business, a nonprofit group, or a government agency. Customer service is the purest kind of right livelihood. And right livelihood is central to the Buddha's path.

Serving others transforms your organization while it transforms the world. If you can take a cranky, unhappy customer and solve his problem, you will transform him into a loyal customer. He, in turn, will tell others about how you helped him, and they will come to you, too. And if you treat them well, they will tell still others, and the word will spread quickly, building your business for you while you just serve people's needs.

Consider how Nordstrom has established a new paradigm for the world of retail, simply by serving superbly, consistently. Consider how Disney has transformed the world of family entertainment, with its theme parks, movies, television programming, and retail stores. Consider how Southwest Airlines has set a new standard for the world of air travel, with its unique style of delivering the basics: low-cost airfare, on-time flights, and peanuts. Everyone in those organizations has just one job: service excellence. If each business and organization took serving others as its number one job, the world would indeed be transformed—and so would their bottom lines!

What Would the Buddha Teach Customer Service People?

It is quite clear that everyone needs peace of mind. The question, then, is how to achieve it. Through anger we cannot; through kindness, through love, through compassion, we can achieve one individual's peace of mind.

—The XIV Dalai Lama, in *The Dalai Lama: A Policy of Kindness*[1]

THE BUDDHA KNOWS customer service is hard work. Customer service is hard because it's so easy to let the negativity of others break down our own mood, our own mind. The Buddha would remind customer service people of the compassionate core of Buddhism and of ourselves. In customer service, our job is to give peace of mind to our customers. We *must* do that through kindness and compassion.

Mindful work is just ordinary work done with a wakeful mind. Nowhere is this more true than in customer service, where you are serving people, helping them solve their problems, taking care of their needs. Here, attitude is everything. You may try to take care of your customers with a mind that is bored, distracted, or resentful; but you will become unhappy, and so will they. Take care of your customers with an attitude of service. You will feel fulfilled in your work, and your customers will be satisfied, too. If you truly do this, the individual who gets peace of mind can be the customer—and can be you as well.

What if you don't feel so great, or you yourself are having a bad day? The Buddha would say, "*Act* your way to a positive mind." Try transforming your unpleasant feelings through pleasant actions. The shortest path is through service. Making your customer's day will make yours.

What Is the Mindful Way to Handle an Angry Customer?

The insults you offer me, though I don't insult you; the taunts you throw at me, though I don't taunt you; the berating you give me, though I don't berate you; all of that I do not take from you. It's all yours, sir. It's all yours! —Samyutta Nikaya 7.2

THE BUDDHA UNDERSTANDS that a customer's anger is almost never personal, even though it is directed at you and might *seem* personal. An angry customer is angry at the situation; you just happen to be the person getting talked to, so naturally you get the anger. In this case, the Buddha emulates the animal realm: he lets the anger roll off his back the way beads of water roll off a duck. Misplaced insults simply don't belong to you; let them go. The customer's anger is not yours, so you don't have to take it and you don't have to respond to it in kind. What a relief! Rejecting anger with a "sir" is so hard! And yet, when you make that leap, it's so perfect, so liberating!

At the same time, the Buddha would not let the customer's *problem* roll off his back. The Buddha's life purpose was to help others, so he would immediately do whatever he could to help the customer. Buddhism is very practical on this level, emphasizing doing the work of the moment.

While the Buddha did not have customers in the sense that our businesses and organizations have them today, as head of a large institution, he did listen to complaints and respond to them. We can use his guidance to create a list of some suggestions he might make for handling an angry customer:

- First, be compassionate. The customer is frustrated, angry, disappointed, and upset. Do not meet anger with anger. Meet anger with compassion. This is powerful practice for you on your own journey.

- Thank the customer for bringing his problem to you. Your mission in mindful work is service, and you cannot be of service if there are no problems to fix. The customer has brought you a gift, an opportunity to help.

- Listen carefully to what the customer is telling you. As you listen, sift through the words and sort out facts from feelings. You must deal with both if you want to make the customer happy again.

- Take notes, if it is appropriate, explaining that you want to make sure you have the information correct so that you can help.

- Emphasize what you *can* do, not what you cannot do. The customer has had plenty of experience with negatives; work from the positives.

- Get help from others if you need it. You may need the assistance of another department, or a coworker, or your boss in order to solve the problem.

- Explain and educate the customer as you continue to interact with him. You may be able to teach things that will enable him to avoid a similar problem in the future.

- Commit to what you can do. Be clear about what the customer can expect and when. Do not commit to something you are uncertain that you can deliver.

- Thank the customer again for the opportunity he gave you to help turn around a negative situation.

- Follow up. Keep your commitments, and keep the customer informed if anything changes.

And remember, problems may be solved, but they are always replaced. They're endless. In the final analysis, your process is your real work.

What Can We Learn from Bad Customer Service?

Aware of the suffering caused by exploitation, social injustice, stealing, and oppression, I vow to cultivate loving-kindness and learn ways to work for the well-being of people, animals, plants, and minerals . . . —The second precept as recited by the Tiep Hien Order

DESPITE THE MYRIAD of books and seminars on customer service, it seems that many individuals and organizations still don't get it. In fact, sometimes it seems as if customer service is becoming worse, not better! Why is this so, and what would the Buddha suggest we do about it as customers and as customer servers?

The Buddha would remind us that most human beings are operating out of ignorance (along with greed and hatred—the three poisons, the three terrible mind-sets leading to all sorts of trouble). They don't see the true nature of things, especially themselves. Their faulty perception leads them to think they are separate from everyone else and need to survive—even if it means screwing someone else. When people are in survival mode, they will use any means necessary to get what they need and want, including exploitation, prejudice, stealing, and oppression. Exactly what the second precept calls us to beware of.

Businesses are like people when it comes to survival. They'll do the same things, and they'll encourage employees to do them as well. Not only will they be duplicitous in their relationships with competitors, but they will even act this way with their customers! This is why we find people who lie to make a sale, warranties riddled with loopholes, business scams, shoddy merchandise, knock-offs sold as genuine, poor-quality workmanship, deceptive advertising, and so on. Survival-at-any-cost thinking comes with a terrible social price, here and all over the world. Business history is replete with examples of greed and exploitation: from the derivative-happy bankers at J.P. Morgan, to Enron and Arthur Andersen, to Ivan Boesky's "greed is healthy," and so on back through the years.

Only by seeing the other as the self can we escape from this cycle of abuse. So, only by seeing the customer as the company can we create a new cycle where both of them respect and please one another. To use a relevant Buddhist metaphor, we are as interconnected as the parts of a car; only when working together do the tires, the frame, the seats, the engine, the steering wheel, have meaning and function. Without that interrelation, there is no car at all. Our customers need us and we need them, just as do the parts of the car. Our response to bad customer service—and to bad business in general—should be to awaken to the vital nature of our interdependence. Giving and getting customer service are not two.

What's the Best Way to Make Your PR Reflect Your Public Relationships?

One addresses those who wish to learn,
without wavering, imparting understanding,
opening up and not obscuring the teaching.
—Anguttara Niyaka 8.16

PUBLIC RELATIONS IS all about speech, and of course right speech is an integral part of the eightfold path. So, public relations workers should epitomize right speech. They also epitomize the organization they work for. Thus, their right speech—which is true, useful, and appropriate—is the organization's speech. It must reflect the organization's mission. We hardly need add that the mission must be value driven and relational.

People (not just PR people) abandon right speech when they are afraid—afraid they will look bad, afraid they will lose something they value, afraid that telling the truth might erode customer regard or market position. Like busy spiders in spiffy suits, they spin webs of stories designed to mask or obscure the truth of a situation. This means that right view—which values relationships above self—has been lost. Working to obscure the truth, right intention and right speech are already out the window, right action follows close behind, and even right livelihood is put in jeopardy. You can see that such efforts abandon nearly the whole eightfold path.

If your public relationships are to be based on trust and respect, you must begin with honesty—in your intent, your speech, and your actions. As soon as you start to spin the truth or dissemble in any way, you have violated the very trust that you say you want with your stakeholders. Don't do it. No matter how bad things are, the cover-up is always worse than any originating problem. History has shown us time and again that organizations that step up and tell the truth, good or bad, reap the benefit of good faith and good will from their customers and everyone else they do business with. That is the basis of solid public relationships. And from our perspective, an organization *is* its relationships, so those relationships must be honest. Honestly, honesty really *is* the best policy.

PART III

❀ Creating a Mindful Workplace

What makes you think work and meditation are two different things?
—Dona Witten and Akong Tulku Rinpoche, *Enlightened Management*[1]

W HO *WOULDN'T* WANT to work in an enlightened workplace? A place where people work hard and feel good about it; a place where trust is high between management and employees; a place of honest, open communication; a place characterized by integrity, personal responsibility, mutual respect, high achievement, personal satisfaction, joy, and great results—isn't that where *everyone* wants to work?

Well, of course—but where does such a place exist, this Pure Land for workers? No need to call a headhunter, scan the want ads, or send out dozens of résumés in hopes of finding a mindful workplace. It isn't *out there*, it's *in here*. It exists where people want it to exist and are willing to work together in creating it for themselves.

How do you start? Start where you are. There is a haunting Zen story of a monk who asks how to enter his path toward enlightenment. His teacher says, "Do you hear the sound of the stream? Enter there." How? It's not a question of *how*, it's a question of *now*.

If you're a manager, supervisor, or executive, you can start by thoroughly assessing your leadership practices, the example you set for others, and the way you manage your people to get the job done. Start where you are.

If you're a nonmanagement employee, start by looking at how you do your own work, how you interact with coworkers and bosses, and especially how you handle problems. Again, start where you are. *Everyone* has a role to play in creating a mindful workplace.

From humble beginnings grow changes that shape organizations. When the Buddha's spirit animates the day-to-day activity of the workplace, the organization inevitably begins to wake up. This is what we mean by mindful work. And an organization where mindful work is getting done begins to change the world. Work is not a values-free zone; it is a profoundly powerful place in which to change the world.

Some of the ideas in this section should open your eyes to where to turn your attention first. Don't wait for someone else to start creating the enlightenment; you may have a very long wait. It is vital that you start. Now.

🧠 Leadership and Bosses

Lead, Follow,
or Get Off the Path

How Can Leaders Develop Their Buddha Nature?

Bodhisattvas become chiefs, captains, priests, governors, even presidents and prime ministers. For the good of the needy they are endless sources of gifts that give rise to the mind of awakening.

—Vimalakirtinirdesha Sutra 8

THE BUDDHA LIVED servant leadership long before today's business book writers and corporate consultants popularized the idea. Leadership metaphors, like management theories, come and go as fads; there's always a program du jour and the temptation to manage by best seller. If you have worked in a large organization and attended a lot of training programs, perhaps you remember some of these: situational leadership, leader as coach, leader as warrior, leader as cheerleader, leader as visionary, leadership heart, leadership soul, Machiavellian leadership, leadership hardball, chainsaw leadership . . . the list is endless.

But who are the leaders we admire most? Who would we most like to follow? Moses, Muhammad, Gandhi, Jesus, Mother Teresa, the Dalai Lama . . . and the Buddha. We think of them because they embody the leadership model in our quote above: servant leadership—leadership in service of the poor, of the disenfranchised, of the hungry, homeless, and hopeless.

Leaders who serve other people are the true leaders, because their leadership goes beyond their organizations and makes a difference in the world. These leaders have given up their egos and executive trappings, and instead chosen the road of simplicity and service. What does the Dalai Lama call himself? "A simple monk." Sure, he has great power and he uses it, but he does not forget that the power belongs to the office, while the feet of clay are his own.

How Can Organizations Identify and Select Good Leaders?

Gray hair doesn't make of you an elder.
That's just age descending on you, dumbly.
When gentle truth and mastery purify and
Awaken you, then you are an elder.

—Dhammapada 260–261

AGE DOES NOT necessarily confer wisdom. As we all know from firsthand experience, youth ends, but immaturity can endure forever!

Good leaders are not necessarily older than their followers, but they are wiser. Leadership is not about chronology; it is about character. The Buddha tells us that to be an elder, respected in the community, one must have traveled the path of discipline, self-reflection, rigorous honesty, and self-control. To be an elder is to be a living example of that path.

Not too many years ago, a Japanese corporate executive, interviewed by an American reporter, described his role as "being the soul of the corporation." He saw himself as the living, breathing embodiment of the values and ethics that were the foundation of his organization. When his followers looked at him, they saw someone putting enlightenment to work.

Perhaps what employees and organizations are yearning for today is a leader who is a chief spiritual officer, not a chief executive officer.

How Does a Great Employer or Boss Embody and Demonstrate His or Her Buddha Nature?

A good employer ministers to her servants and employees in five ways: by assigning them work they can manage; by giving them food and money; by supporting them in sickness; by sharing special delicacies; and by granting them leave when appropriate.

—Digha Nikaya 31

THE BUDDHA KNEW that no matter what kind of organization you run, it is smart to be as good an employer as you can. When there's plenty of labor, the best and the brightest will want to work for you. And when there's a shortage of labor, you will still be able to choose the best and retain them.

Being a great employer is not some mysterious, complex thing; it's about getting the basics right. The Buddha lists five:

1. Assign work that employees can manage. Make sure that job requirements are a good fit with employees' skills and abilities; make sure they have appropriate education and training. Also build enough challenge into each job to maintain employees' interest. This may be difficult to do with some jobs, but give it some thought and be resourceful. Things like cross-training, job enrichment, job enlargement, job rotation, and special projects will help keep people challenged, engaged, and committed.

2. Give employees food and money. Larger employers provide a company cafeteria, and smaller ones have lunchrooms with refrigerators and microwaves. Productivity and health are directly related. You must pay employees well and care for them if you expect them to care for you and the work.

3. Support employees in sickness. Everyone gets sick once in a while; and when people are sick, they need special care. If you give them that care, they will gratefully return it many times over when they come back to work.

4. Share special delicacies. A little something extra every so often is a wonderful way to let people know you appreciate them and their good work; sharing the goodies, whether profits or in some other form, is highly reinforcing.

5. Grant employees leave when appropriate. People are not cogs in a machine and cannot be treated as such. Special circumstances require benevolence and flexibility in allowing time away from work, whether for maternity leave, family care, a sabbatical to refresh and recharge, or other personal needs.

What does it take to be a great boss or employer? The Buddha has laid out the basics. By all means, add to this list, but don't miss the boat by missing the basics.

Why Do Some Bosses Surround Themselves with Yes-Men (or Yes-Women)?

A flatterer is an enemy pretending to be a friend in four phases: he approves of your bad choices; he disapproves of your good choices; he praises you whenever you're around; then he blames you when you're not. —Digha Nikaya 31

WE FIND YES-MEN (and yes-women) everywhere, especially in organizations where decisions are made not so much on facts and figures as on personalities and politics. Insecure bosses will often reward such people. They let it be known that they don't want anyone to disagree with them or question their decisions.

There may come a time when you are tempted to become a yes-person. Resist this temptation for at least two reasons. First, when you do this, you will not only lose your self-respect, but you'll likely lose the respect of your peers (who see what you're up to) and, ultimately, the person whose ass you bent over to kiss (even if they asked for it, they will not reward you for long). This is a good enough reason, though shortsighted.

The second reason is that even if you are willing to sacrifice your integrity this way, and your boss keeps eating it up, the strategy cannot be sustained. Without candid and accurate feedback from team members and employees, even a powerful boss loses perspective and makes poor choices. Projects fail. When you tie yourself to such a boss, you tie yourself to a sinking ship. Sure, you can blame your boss for these failures, but you're still there, sinking along with him. Further, you're sinking your whole organization, along with all the good it might be doing for all sentient beings. Now *that* is reason enough.

How Can You Be Buddha at Work If You Have a Tough, Demanding Boss?

See a critic as a treasure map;
Stay around and things always get better.
Let him teach and wean you from wrong action.
Good people learn to love him, others don't.
—Dhammapada 76–77

TEACHERS WHO DEMAND the most of their students help their students to grow the most. It's the same with bosses. Employees rise highest when they rise under bosses who set high standards and challenging goals for them. Employees with bosses who expect mediocre performance usually give it to them. Worse yet are lax and undemanding bosses; they're doing you a real disservice by selling you short.

The Buddha knows that a worker with a tough boss is like an athlete with a tough coach—that worker, and that athlete, will work harder, stretch his or her capabilities, and reach new levels of achievement. Yes, it's hard to remember this when a tough boss pushes you out of your comfort zone, but just as the Buddha says, stick with this boss, because he's guiding you to treasure. (Remember, here we're talking about a tough boss, not a terrible boss. That's another topic; see below.)

Think of your boss's criticisms and instructions as his expressions of love for you and concern for your future. (And even if your boss is just a tyrant who doesn't love you, you can still be mindful at your job and see what there is to learn from such a boss. Hint: sometimes we learn best from those who demonstrate what *not* to do and how *not* to be.)

Ken Blanchard (a.k.a. "The One Minute Manager") says, "Feedback is the breakfast of champions." If your boss never tells you what you're doing wrong, how can you improve? If you're a good employee, you'll learn to love it (or at least respect it, even if you don't love it). If you're not learning this, it's time to rethink yourself, not your boss.

Do Successful Executives Always Have Big Egos?

A fool who knows he is foolish is wise in that;
A fool who thinks he's wise fulfills the name.
—Dhammapada 63

JACK WELCH, CEO of General Electric for 20 years, used to say, "If you're not confused, you don't know what's going on." That's such a superbly Buddhist observation. Those who pretend to be masters of the situation are fooling themselves. Better to admit your unknowing. Shunryu Suzuki Roshi used to say he didn't know what he was doing, running an enormous Zen center. People thought he was being humble, but he was admitting the simple truth.

Wise people are humble people—they *know* they don't know. People with big egos are foolish people—they *don't* know they don't know. They are ignorant of their own ignorance; they are fools who think themselves wise. Thus, they are doubly foolish.

Better to be humble, like Jack Welch. If he was confused, he was acknowledging humility. He was always a beginner.

The Buddha reminds us to be conscious of our own foolishness. Own and acknowledge the fact that there is much you don't know. The place of unknowing is not a bad place to be in—it means you are teachable and open to learning. You can't be teachable and maintain a big ego at the same time. Suzuki Roshi wrote a lovely book, *Zen Mind, Beginner's Mind*, teaching us how to maintain the freshness of beginners. Both he and Jack Welch also retained the humbleness of beginners. Good enough for them, good enough for you.

What Happens When Leaders Get into Power Struggles?

He brings together the divided, he encourages friends.
He is a peacemaker, loving peace, passionate for peace,
speaking words that bring peace.

—Anguttara Nikaya 10.176

POWER STRUGGLES ARISE out of the illusion of separateness that we live in. We need a healthy ego to survive, but when the ego forgets its own contingent nature, it moves us to struggle for power and pleasure as if these were the only important things. Anyone engaged in a power struggle has lost his mind—his Buddha mind.

A workplace is not, fundamentally, a place of separateness. When rival leaders act as if it is, the best you can do is stay out of the way. You don't want to become a casualty of their turf tussle. Do your work well; do not take sides; don't gossip or speculate with coworkers; keep out of the line of fire as the warring parties duke it out. You may be enlisted by one or *both* sides in the war. Be a conscientious objector. If people are really listening, you might mention that not only is struggle for power unsustainable, but domination is unsustainable as well. Tell them that since an organization functions fully only in peace, you'll be preserving your peace with both sides. But tell them just once. They may actually hear you later; for now, as always, you have your own challenges.

How Can You Maintain Your Peace of Mind If You Work for a Terrible Boss?

Treating others the way he's treating me,
He'll be destroyed and then I shall be free.
—Jataka 278

WE HEAR ONE reassuring refrain again and again as we study the Buddha's teachings: what goes around comes around. Even a bad boss will get his comeuppance. We never know in advance what the karmic punishment will look like or when it will come, but we can rest assured that it will come. Perhaps he'll mess with the wrong employee and end up being sued. Perhaps his deeds will come to the attention of his own bosses, and they'll fire him. Perhaps his employees will unite against him and find subtle ways of turning the tables. But mainly, he will always pay the highest price: he will surround himself with *dukkha*.

The important thing here is to remember that it is not *your* job to even the score. You are not to take on the role of judge and jury with your boss, even if he's bad enough to make you want to. You are not the hammer of karma. Stay out of your boss's and take care of your own. Do a good job at your work; be compassionate and cooperative with coworkers; try to stay out of harm's way and minimize any contact you have to have with your boss;

be respectful when you do have to deal with him. This is exactly what the Buddha knows and does. He doesn't soil himself with retribution; he doesn't have to. In the worst case, quit working for your terrible boss. What does that pain gain you?

This is a serious question, one with both external and internal answers. Externally, others have trouble with him; if you can work with him, you are rare and people will notice. Internally, if you *really* want to be a good student of the Buddha and are willing to take on a difficult learning assignment, we have a radical suggestion: *love* your terrible boss. He's a nasty teacher, but he can teach you lessons that your friends never can.

Having a terrible boss is one of those situations we find ourselves in more often than we'd like, but there is often a powerful spiritual lesson available in these awful situations. Look for what there is to learn; see what qualities you can cultivate in yourself while you're in this situation. Someday you may look back and realize that you became stronger and more resilient, patient, kind, and compassionate as a result of working for a jerk.

✿ The Big Issues

Beyond the Bottom Line

Is There Any Conflict between Being a Buddha at Work and Making a Profit?

Beginning with only a little cash,
The wise can skillfully cause it to grow,
Like the slowly building wind can cause
A spark to grow into a mighty fire.

—Jataka 4

PEOPLE OFTEN IMAGINE the Buddha as an otherworldly ascetic who thinks we should renounce money and the material world. It is true that the Buddha did this, but he hardly expected everyone to do the same. He didn't want the world to fall apart. He was very much in favor of making a profit, provided that it was done in keeping with the basic principles of awakening: honesty, integrity, personal responsibility, right livelihood, cooperation, harmony, and so on. In fact, making a profit with mindful business practices would be a perfect example of Buddhism in action. Remember, the dharma is, above all, practical, teaching us how to live and work in the real world. You can't get more real than the world of work.

The wise person, one who follows the Buddha's teachings about skillful practice, can build his or her business slowly, steadily, as one would build a fire. By all means, get a nice little blaze of profit building there. You can toast some mighty tasty marshmallows over such a fire.

Replacing Bottom-Line Thinking with
Buddha-Mind Thinking

He was honored as the businessman among businessmen because
he showed the priority of truth. —Vimalakirtinirdesha Sutra 2

THE BUDDHA TAUGHT balance. Buddhism is not called "the middle path" for nothing. So, what is balance in organizational life? The bottom line measures short-term profit, but this is only one measure of a company's strength and vitality. A business might be making lots of money but still have blind spots and weak links that undermine its sustainability.

Here we encounter another instance of contemporary best business practices taking a cue from Buddhism. Some of today's smarter businesses use a "balanced scorecard" to make comprehensive assessments of organizational health and effectiveness. This approach follows a middle way between profits and such things as customer satisfaction, innovation, and employee learning. Your organization will want to determine what factors are important to you, and then design ways to measure and evaluate those factors. Taking this holistic approach to organizational strength will help ensure that your enterprise sustains itself into the future.

How Do You Bring Your Buddha Mind to the Task of Writing a Good Mission Statement?

I am not satisfied simply doing hard work and carrying out the affairs of state. I believe my real duty is the welfare of the whole world, and doing hard work and carrying out the affairs of state are just its foundation. —King Ashoka, Sixth Rock Edict

KING ASHOKA WAS perhaps the greatest Buddhist ruler in history. He established a dynasty in India, over two thousand years ago. He began with force, but he converted to Buddhism and changed his mission. He saw there was no point in ruling over a great kingdom that did not serve the people. He realized that his true duty—his dharma, which means his truth as well as his job description—went beyond strengthening the government; it went even beyond his country. His dharma was to provide a vision of welfare for all the world. That is why, though his dynasty has vanished, his values continue to work for the welfare of the whole world.

Heading a company is like this. In the final analysis, our mission is not merely to work hard and carry out business affairs. These are only the means of achieving our *real* mission, which should always be the welfare of the whole world. Of course, like Ashoka, we need to take care of the foundation; we can't build without a foundation. But a foundation is pointless unless we build something real and lasting on it. Visionary businesspeople know this; they feel the deep need for this; they feel this as their dharma. And they give the world innovations that better our lives.

For instance, the mission of Disney is "to make people happy." The company is committed to the happiness of all people everywhere because it knows that its customers come from every part of the world—and there are many more generations of customers to come. People are willing to pay for experiences and products that make them feel happy, and this results in a robust bottom line for Disney. But the Buddha would say that the bottom line should never be the primary mission; the bottom line is the by-product of the primary mission: making people happy.

How Does the Buddha Invest in the Future?

A treasure stored in a deep pit makes no profit and is easily lost. Real treasure is gathered through charity, piety, moderation, self-control, and good deeds. It is securely kept and cannot be lost.
—Vinaya Mahavagga 4

LOOKING AT THESE words philosophically, we can see the echo of all great spiritual teachers: the true treasure is love, not gold. The Buddha knew this, too, and we all know this deep inside ourselves.

We can also look at these words as an endorsement of values-based business practices. The Buddha is clearly in favor of the idea of making a profit, but he encourages us to make our profit in the right way, with solid values and ethical behavior. Warren Buffett (a billionaire with good values) and many other successful business leaders today would concur with the Buddha.

An enterprise that hoards all its resources greedily will soon find itself with no public goodwill, no partners among other businesses, and employees who feel disheartened and exploited. On the other hand, an enterprise that builds partnerships with other businesses, treats employees as valued partners in the business, sees itself as a responsible member of the surrounding community, and shares its resources with the poor and needy will be an organization that is built to last. Customers will be loyal, as will employees. The treasure of goodwill will be there in good times and in bad. The Buddha knows that an enterprise such as this understands that doing well and doing good go hand in hand.

How Can You Create and Develop a Mindful, Learning Organization?

With work comes wisdom; without work, no wisdom.
Know the path and work to increase wisdom.

—Dhammapada 282

I F THE BUDDHA were around today, he would be likely to use a vivid metaphor to bring the importance of continuous growth and learning to life. "Consider the shark," the Buddha might say, "who must constantly move forward or die. He must keep moving through the water, so that the water will move through him, bringing him oxygen, keeping him alive. So too does your organization need to keep moving, or it will die. Learning is endless, and the more you know, the more you realize how much you don't know. The moment your organization ceases to be a learning organization, in that moment it begins to die."

Here's a story told by contemporary teachers Christina Feldman and Jack Kornfield in their book *Stories of the Spirit, Stories of the Heart*:

> One day Mara, the Evil One, was travelling through the villages of India with his attendants. He saw a man doing walking meditation whose face was lit up in wonder. The man had just discovered something on the ground in front of him.
>
> Mara's attendant asked what that was and Mara replied, "A piece of truth."
>
> "Doesn't this bother you when someone finds a piece of truth, O Evil One?" his attendant asked.
>
> "No," Mara replied. "Right after this, they usually make a belief out of it."[1]

We should conduct ourselves so that wisdom will grow. Our organization's structures should be designed to facilitate learning at all levels, in all areas, even if at first we don't see the relevance.

Professional development opportunities including seminars, university programs, special project teams, and mentoring programs are just a few examples of structured learning.

Our policies and procedures should be written and implemented to encourage continuous learning, even though this might upset our schedules. Generous tuition reimbursement policies demonstrate that we value learning at all levels; we are literally putting our money where our mouth is.

Our workspaces should be arranged so that we can easily get together and learn from one another. There should be ample places for people to gather and share ideas and experiences. Set up a white board by the water cooler. Create alcoves and equip them with flip charts so that people can exchange information. And organizational leaders must lead the way, always themselves learning and developing their wisdom.

Upaya *is about unlimited possibilities. It is analyzing the situation from every angle and simply letting your intuition be your guide. When you set your mind to accomplishing a task, and then truly open yourself up to finding a way to do it, everything becomes a Buddha. All people, places, and situations seem to be guiding and conspiring for your success.*
—Kiley Jon Clark

FOR THE BUDDHA, this is an easy answer: *begin where you are, work with what you have, and create from there.* This is *upaya*, skillful means. You have plenty of intelligence, talent, imagination, resourcefulness, and creativity inside of you—work with it. Kiley Jon Clark works with the homeless at HMP Street Dharma. If upaya works for them, it can work for you.

While it is good to look around to see what others are doing or have done in the past, and to be inspired by them, do not *copy* them. Judy Garland is reported to have told her daughter Liza Minnelli, "Be a first-rate version of yourself, not a second-rate version of someone else." She ought to know.

Begin where you are. The Buddha never tired of trying to wake us up to the world around us—that's the whole point of mindfulness, no? Keep your eyes and ears open as you go through your day. Listen to what people are talking about; they are constantly giving you clues about what is important to them and what interests them—sometimes in ways they don't even notice. Being mindful of where they go (in complaining, in sharing, in the physical plant), you can spot needs that haven't been met and be inspired to find new products, services, and processes to meet those needs.

Work with what you have. Do not artificially limit your mind! Always question your assumptions and beliefs; they may be blinding you to opportunities for innovation and creativity. If you find yourself (or others) saying, "That's impossible," think again. What is "impossible" today may be very possible tomorrow.

Create from there. Practice divergent thinking. The human mind is capable of two kinds of problem solving: convergent and divergent. Convergent thinking is what you use to find a single correct answer to a question—for example, in math, logic, and historical dating. Divergent thinking is what you use to find several emergent possible answers to a problem or question—for example, finding alternative routes to get downtown. You are born with the ability to engage in both types of thinking, but our one-size-fits-all education system overwhelmingly encourages and rewards convergent thinking. So we often have to relearn how to brainstorm, explore options, look beyond the obvious, and question those who say there is only one right way. Creativity flourishes when people—and organizations—give themselves permission not only to think outside the box, but to tear the box apart and reassemble it in new ways. This is just what serious meditators do with their brains. In both ways, the Buddha says to reject business as usual and think for yourself.

What Do Mindful Leaders Do to Foster Corporate Responsibility?

A bodhisattva does not give food and drink to gluttons and drunkards. . . . And though it's his own wealth, if those he's responsible for are distressed when he gives it away, he doesn't do it. —The Precious Jewel of the Teaching 12, quoting the Ratnavali

HOW MUCH SHOULD a business leader give to charity? A significant chunk? A token amount? Here the Buddhist teachings remind us that a business leader's best contribution may be in putting money back into the company. After all, charity begins at home. When Bill Gates and Ted Turner gave away billions of dollars, some criticized them for neglecting their primary obligation to their own companies and the wealth those companies could create for their shareholders. Did they go against the Buddha's teaching?

The Buddha says two wise things about giving. First, one should never give money or things to those who would misuse them. We know this already, but it is sometimes hard to resist such giving, since people may clamor loudly for our gift or may try to induce guilt if we resist. But we must be firm in our resolve. Giving must go to those who will use the gift well. There are so many worthwhile, deserving recipients to choose from today that we must make sure we do not squander our generosity by giving poorly.

The text gives us another wise word: One must be careful not to harm one's own company in one's charity. After all, it is employees who generate the wealth through their hard work, and it is shareholders who invest their money in the company's future. It is inappropriate to be generous with outsiders if one has not first been generous with insiders. Certainly, if it harms employees or the health of the organization (even indirectly, through employee resentment or shareholder bad feelings), one should not give away a company's wealth, no matter how worthy the recipient.

Giving is a fundamental virtue, but we must think of the larger picture when we give. Does the recipient really gain? Will others be inadvertently hurt in the process? The answers are not always easy; this is why we must ask the questions.

What Would the Buddha Think of the Business Trend of "Going Green"?

When you throw away your spit and toothbrushes,
You must hide them well away from sight.
Dumping waste in places that we share
And in the water system leads to ill.

—Bodhicharyavatara 5.91

FOR THE BUDDHA, it's just as true at work as at home: we must treat the places we share with respect, and with seven billion people on the planet, *every* place is a place we share.

To give a concrete example, your organization's policies on paper recycling have the power to go far beyond its walls, because they create public perceptions and markets. This is especially true if you work for a large corporation. When a few large companies make the change to recycling paper and to buying recycled paper even for reports, proposals, and correspondence, many other companies will take notice. When many companies make this change, they will create a market that will change the economics of scale in recycled paper and drive the price down. Finally, we'll all be so comfortable with recycled paper that we'll wonder why people ever wanted paper bleached to blinding whiteness. Then we'll at last follow the Bodhicharyavatara's words and stop dumping dioxin into the water system.

Recycling and using recycled paper is relatively simple, just one aspect of addressing an organization's carbon footprint. But what works with recycling also works with lighting, transportation, building materials and locations, and so on—all the complex of things, actions, and relationships that create a carbon footprint. Change might start with one person in the company who keeps bringing up recycling at meetings until something gets done. Corporate responsibility does not necessarily start at the top. It can start with anyone who has the courage, patience, and persistence to be a voice of integrity and to keep speaking until others take up the chorus and join you.

🕉 Work Practices and Processes

Practice Is Awakening

How Can a Mindful Leader Develop Long-Term Perspectives?

The farmer ploughs and plants his field well. But a farmer has no magic power to command "Today let my crops sprout up. Tomorrow let the grains come forth. The day after let them ripen." No, only time can make this happen.
—Anguttara Nikaya 3.91

MOST EASTERN CULTURES traditionally take a much longer view of time than Western cultures. These views are rooted in religion. The Buddha shared the Indian long-term perspective on time. He understood that character development is a lifelong process (or even longer!), and that patience and persistence are its keys. This is also true of many aspects of organizational life. We are often planting seeds whose fruits lie months or years away.

Everything has a season. You cannot control the seasons, nor can you rush them. And so it is at work. Some work activities yield results quickly, while others are long-term endeavors. Both are important, but if there is an area where most of us are lacking, it is in long-term thinking. Many of us want instant gratification: we want to see results right away. We dig up our carrots every week to see if they are growing. We are an impatient lot.

The Buddha counsels us to develop patience; it is one of the ten perfections that Mahayana Buddhists strive to embody. Learn to trust that all endeavors yield appropriate fruits in their own time. Notice we didn't say "your time," but theirs.

How Does the Buddha Mind Design Effective Work Processes?

Gathering reeds and branches and binding them into a raft, he crosses to the safety of the other shore, depending on the raft and the effort of his hands and feet. Having crossed over he thinks, "How useful this raft has been! . . . Why don't I carry it on my back as I go where I want?" What do you think, monks: in doing this, is the man doing the right thing with the raft? —Majjhima Nikaya 22

THE BUDDHA KNOWS how easily we humans become attached. We become attached to all kinds of things, including the work processes we're familiar with. If something has worked for us in the past (the raft), we cling to it long after it becomes a burden. Often we're not even aware that we don't need it anymore. We fall into habit, doing things the way we have always done them. It is comfortable, familiar, and easy.

In business, this is an especially tricky problem if we have been successful until now but don't know exactly why. This is superstitious learning—fearing that if we change anything, we will screw up our successes. For instance, a baseball player wears his lucky socks; a performer has her little pre-performance ritual; a student transcribes her notes in her special notebook, in order to maintain her straight-A average. If something has worked for us in the past, we are loath to let go of it even if we *know* we don't need it now. We might need it again in the future . . . hey, that future could be now; letting go of it might *create* the dreaded need for it; oh yeah, we had best hold on to it. Ah, attachment, the root of all suffering.

The Buddha is consistent in all his teachings: let it all go. Everything is changing—always has been, always will be. Continually look at your work processes in light of today's work, not yesterday's. If you are still holding on to processes that add no value, then you are burdening yourself (and your organization) uselessly. Be awake: when you've reached land, drop the raft. Overhaul your work processes as often as is necessary to stay current.

How Do We Bring Our Mindfulness to Technology?

Before you start and after you finish working, make this one simple gesture toward your computer: Give it a nod . . .

Some people might balk at the idea of showing respect to a machine. Doesn't that imply subservience, they ask? Besides, the machine acts so impetuously, who can respect it? Why show respect to something so arbitrary and unreliable?

Because it gives to us.

—Philip Toshio Sudo, *Zen Computer*[1]

THE BUDDHA WOULD welcome any technology that improves our lives. Like any tool—a hammer, a chemical, a knife—a tool is not good or bad in and of itself. It is just a tool, an object we can use for good or bad purposes. If it does good things, the Buddha welcomes it, so the Buddha would support ongoing technological development.

When we show respect for people, they are more likely to live up to it. They are also likely to respect us in return. Perhaps it is also so with computers and other forms of technology: when we respect them and treat them well, they are more likely to work well for us. They even seem more likely to respect us.

Our computers may not have minds (though there are days when we swear they *do* have minds—evil ones), but they are indeed slowly progressing toward consciousness. For now, when we treat them with respect for how they improve our lives, we begin to create a reality where they *do* improve our lives.

Respect does not imply subservience; it implies an affirmation of goodness. If a technology gives to us, let us acknowledge and encourage it. This will help us control the technology mindfully and keep doing good with it. If we bow to our meditation cushions (and Buddhists do), we surely can bow to our computers.

Business Gurus and Consultants

Whether you're looking inside or outside, whatever you find,
you've got to destroy it. If you find a Buddha, kill the Buddha.

—The Record of Linji 19

WHAT'S THE DEFINITION of a consultant? A consultant is one who borrows your watch and then tells you what time it is. The Buddha would like this definition. He would tell you to "kill" the consultants—not literally, of course (by the way, please don't literally kill Buddhas you meet, either), but kill off the awe and reverence with which you slavishly follow them. The Buddha did not have a Harvard PhD, nor did he wear pin-striped suits or carry a business card from McKinsey. And even if he did, as a genuine Buddha, he would tell you to think for yourself.

Yes, you might need some help, someone to be a resource for you in solving problems, exploring alternatives, and creating new opportunities. But don't ever change how you run your department or your organization simply because an authority tells you to. A good consultant is like a doctor: he can diagnose your problems, he can assess your strengths, and he can provide you with information and resources to help you get better. But ultimately *you* are the one who is going to eat healthy foods, do the physical therapy, get rest, take the right medicines at the right times, and mobilize your resources to get healthy. *You* are the one who's going to do the work and do the healing. No one can do it for you, even if he does have a best-selling business book on the *New York Times* list. So don't hang on to authority, even the Buddha's.

How Can You Cultivate Mindful Communication within Your Organization?

He speaks when it's appropriate, with truth, wisdom, and restraint.
He speaks only when it's right, and speaks only what is profitable,
well-supported, clear, and effective.   —Anguttara Nikaya 10.176

THE BUDDHA PRACTICED good communication and created rules to forbid bad communication (gossip, idle chatter, saying hurtful things to someone or about someone) in the sangha. Monastics do not indulge in these things, and neither should co-workers. Individuals should exercise self-restraint and good judgment in how they communicate with one another. Likewise, an organization would do well to engage in communication that is meaningful, well supported, clear, and effective.

Communication seems like such a simple thing on the surface, yet most organizations can't seem to do it well. Consider: when employees are asked how they would prefer to get their information, the overwhelming majority of them report that they want it directly from their immediate boss. Their second preferred source of information is team meetings. But when asked how they *do* receive most of their information, employees report that their number one source is the company "grapevine" (gossip), and second is written memos—the least preferred sources!

The Buddha would make leaders speak directly to employees. That is what he did, and he mandated it in his own organization. The Buddha would start some good ol' face-to-face conversation, either one-on-one or in groups. He would warn us to resist the urge to communicate important information on a mass scale, through company-wide e-mails, memos, or newsletters. As a rule, with communication, the more impersonal, the less effective. The Buddha was clearly a high-touch kind of guy, not high-tech. E-mail, faxes, memos, and bulletin boards all have their place, of course, but the Buddha knew that there was something special about the personal touch. He knew that nothing beats clear, effective, honest communication between human beings.

How Do You Conduct a Mindful Meeting?

First, the passion for analysis and knowing defiles the Buddha Nature. Second, the passion for emotions and desires defiles the Buddha Nature. —The Lion's Roar of Queen Shrimala 3

EVERYONE KNOWS THAT meetings get bogged down in many ways. A group meeting is a lot like the human mind, filled with conflicting desires, energy and impulses, short-term and long-term goals, digressions and distractions. What covers up the mind's original purity is not so different from what covers up the original purity of a well-intentioned meeting. Two distinct types of passions derail meetings: the passion for analysis and the passion for emotions.

The passion for analysis and knowing is commonly referred to as "analysis paralysis" and is familiar to anyone who has worked in a large organization. But even small groups of people can fall victim to this passion. Analysis and knowledge are somewhat deceptive, because on the surface they make it look as if something is happening and the group is doing its work. Yet if you watch carefully over time, you will see that a group overcome with this passion is simply going in circles, unproductively rehashing the same material, searching in vain for reassurance that a mistake will not be made and that success is a sure thing. Once the group is on this track, the more analysis and the less clarity it has. The group debates and analyzes for so long that the window of opportunity for action closes, and it becomes too late to do anything. The group has analyzed itself right into inaction.

Other meetings become ineffective through the passion for emotions. People in the grip of this passion desire an intensity of emotion that will empower the group, but they allow what begins as rational debate to escalate into irrational argument. All ability for good judgment can be lost, and discussion of issues and facts devolves into personal attack. Passions run high, tempers flare, people say harsh things they will regret later, and the group spins out of control into conflict and chaos. The result is either inaction or wrong action taken in the heat of the moment.

The Buddha tells us to beware of both too much rational analysis and too much irrational emotion. Both are extremes that lead to bad ends. The Buddha would have an agenda for his meeting, but he would also deviate from it if the discussion seemed to be going in a fruitful direction. He would make sure that everyone had a chance to be heard, and he would encourage quiet people to open up and share their thoughts on the issues at hand. Still waters often run deep, so we mustn't let strong, verbal personalities dominate the discussion. Buddha would make sure that everyone at the meeting understood his guidelines: right speech, right intention, and so forth. He would respect everyone's time by starting and ending his meeting at the appointed hours. Wisdom and compassion are the order of the day—in meetings as in life.

The Care and Feeding of Employees

Your Team as Your Sangha

How Do We Bring Mindfulness to the Process of Selection and Hiring?

Until you've come to know the spiritual state of living beings, don't assume anything about the shape of their abilities. Do not wound the healthy. Do not force those wishing to walk the wide world onto a narrow path. Do not try to pour the deep ocean into a cow's hoofprint. . . . Do not confuse the glow of a glowworm for the light of the sun. And do not force those who love the roar of a lion to listen to the cry of a jackal!
—Vimalakirtinirdesha Sutra 3

APPEARANCES CAN BE very deceiving, especially when it comes to human beings! The Buddha is saying here that unless you've done the work that hiring takes, you just might judge a book by its cover. Big mistake.

Most organizations waste enormous amounts of time, money, and energy cleaning up the mistakes they have made by hiring people without due diligence. Far too many managers still hire on the basis of "a gut feeling" that an applicant has the requisite skills. Far too little attention is paid to checking out the job applicant's work history, ability to learn and grow, and, most important, ability to work well with other people.

It is common knowledge that people get hired for their technical skills; they get promoted for innovation; and they get fired for their trouble with interpersonal skills. Fully 80 percent of people who fail on the job fail because they can't get along with their coworkers, boss, customers, or all of the above.

So how would the Buddha select and hire the right person for the job? The Buddha didn't exactly hire people—he attracted followers, people who wanted to learn from him and follow his example. But understanding the Buddha's teachings can still give us some idea of how he might go about hiring if he were working in an organization today.

The Buddha would begin *inside*, using his mind to clarify what kind of person he was looking for and wanted to attract. He would include both character and competence in his thinking. He would set the stage to attract someone with good values and integrity, someone who was walking his own spiritual path. And he would create an environment that would attract someone who had the necessary skills to do the job, or who could learn those skills.

Then, the Buddha would tap into all we have learned through human resources research on job success factors—he would take advantage of the experience and wisdom of those who have studied job applicants and their performance track records. The Buddha was methodical, not a man driven by whim and impulse. He would do his homework and approach the job of hiring in a methodical way. Here are some of the steps he might advise us to take:

- Make sure you have a good pool of applicants by casting your net as widely as possible. Don't limit your search to obvious candidates.

- Be clear about what is required in the job. Make a list of the duties and tasks. Make a list of the results you want achieved. Make a list of desirable personal characteristics.

- Consider what it takes to be successful in your particular organization and/or department. Think about people who are successful, and list the behaviors and character traits that make them successful. The new person needs to be a good match for your organizational culture.

- Involve many people in the interview process. Others will see things that you miss or overlook.

- Ask behavioral questions. The best predictor of future performance is past performance. Ask tough questions: "Describe a time when you had to deal with a difficult customer. How did you do it?" "Tell me about an instance in which you made a serious mistake. How did you fix it?" Questions like these get at real-life behavior and uncover the candidate's values and character.

- Don't use hypothetical questions. Anyone can make up an easy answer to a question like "How would you handle a supply-side problem?" People spin nice stories when they project themselves into hypothetical situations, but these answers have little or nothing to do with reality.

- Make sure the candidate also has an opportunity to ask lots of questions. Hiring should be a two-way process. You can learn as much about a candidate from questions she asks as you can from the answers she gives.

- Don't be in a hurry to hire. Haste in the beginning can be costly later on.

- Use job tests wherever you can, whether it's a typing test, a computer simulation, a role-playing scenario, or some other test designed to assess applicants' skills and abilities.

- In addition to looking at a candidate's *past* performance, be sure to consider her *future* potential. Ask about generic skills: budgeting, organizing, solving problems, writing, making presentations, coming up with new ideas, cutting costs, working well with others, and so on. The candidate may not have done the particular job you are interviewing her for, but if she has the right generic skills, she can do it successfully. Smart employers hire with an eye to the candidate's future potential, not just her past experience.

- Be sure you are honest with the candidate about the nature of the job as well as future growth potential. You don't want to misrepresent a job to the candidate and have her quit in disappointment later on.

- Finally, look especially carefully at someone who interviews well or tries to get away with glib answers to questions. She may be skilled at interviewing, but make sure that she also has the other skills to back up her brilliant interviews. Due diligence is essential: listen carefully, watch how she behaves when she is nervous, ask her tough questions, work to discern her true character.

Yes, all this is time-consuming. But either you can put in the time on the front end of the relationship, or you can spend the time later dealing with discipline, coaching, retraining—even firing and then having to hire someone new.

What Really Motivates People?

> *Once I was staying with my mother in London. At the time she was the housekeeper for a very wealthy Canadian who lived in a luxury flat just off Hyde Park. They all went off for a while, and I had the flat to myself. There I was in London, living in this luxurious flat with two huge color television sets and all the food I could possibly eat! I had enough money for whatever I wanted, lots of records, lots of everything. But I was so bored!*
>
> *I told myself, "Please remember this. If you are ever tempted to think that physical comfort gives happiness, remember this."*
>
> *But then, another time I was staying in a cave, not my cave but another cave, which was very small. It was so small that you couldn't stand up in it, with a tiny box you could only just sit in, and that was the bed as well. It was full of fleas, so I was covered in flea bites. You had to go half a mile down a very steep track to bring up water. There was also almost no food at all, and it was hot. But I was in bliss. I was so happy. It was a very holy place, and the people there were wonderful. Although from a physical point of view the situation was difficult, so what! The mind was happy. I remember that whole place as being bathed in golden light. Do you see what I mean?*
>
> —Ani Tenzin Palmo, *Reflections on a Mountain Lake*[1]

MANY BOSSES WANT to motivate their people but feel frustrated because they don't have money to spend on bonuses and pay-for-performance salary increases. No matter how many times you tell them, "Money isn't everything," they don't believe it. Yet it's true: money is vastly overrated as a motivator.

Tenzin Palmo's personal story illustrates the findings of Frederick Herzberg, who conducted what has become classic research on worker motivation. Herzberg's research revealed that while the *absence* of material rewards such as money and perks may *de*-motivate people, these things offer no guarantee of *motivating* them. The effects of pay raises and bonuses last only weeks, because people just adjust their spending, and their positive feelings wear off. Herzberg learned that what really motivates people are intangibles: appreciation and recognition by their peers and the boss, interesting work, challenging tasks that offer stimulation and learning, autonomy and flexibility, and meaning and purpose in work. This is why missionaries, social workers, teachers, nurses, firefighters, and others who receive low pay and work in dirty or difficult circumstances still work so hard. They're motivated by their participation in a job and a field that *gives*.

What Role Do Expectations Play in Personal and Organizational Success?

Before the battle of Okehazama, General Oda Nobunaga, though highly outnumbered, was confident. Still, he knew his men had doubts. They stopped at a Shinto shrine and Nobunaga told them, "After we pray to the gods for help, I will toss a coin. If it comes up heads, we will surely win. If tails, we will lose. Our fate depends on the gods." When he tossed the coin, it came up heads. Assured of the gods' favor, his soldiers were eager to fight.

Nobunaga's small army did win. In fact, they eventually united the entire country. After their victory, the men were jubilant, and one of Nobunaga's lieutenants pronounced, "No one can change destiny." "No indeed," said Nobunaga, revealing a coin with heads on both sides.
—Popular Japanese Zen story

SOME PEOPLE SAY, "I'll believe it when I see it." The human truth is closer to "I'll see it when I believe it." Buddhist teachings arise from and reflect back on the power of our mind. Thoughts become things; beliefs become reality; our nightmares come true—as do our dreams. Choose your thoughts and beliefs wisely; with them you are literally creating your own future. And, as Nobunaga's example teaches us, you might be creating the future of an entire corporation or an entire nation. In yourself and in others, create positive mind-sets, and you create the possibility of success.

How Can Buddhist Training Inform Business Training?

Do not think that I intended to create a "teaching system" to help
people learn the way. Do not hold such a view. What I teach is
the truth I have found. A "teaching system" means nothing because
truth can't be divided into pieces and rearranged in a system.

—Diamond Sutra 6

A GAIN AND AGAIN, the Buddha resists our efforts to pin him or his teaching down into a neat little system. He knows how much we long for security and reassurance in a world that is constantly changing. We want him to give us those "Seven Easy Steps to Enlightenment" or "Top Ten Ways to Get Nirvana Now." Just check out the best-seller lists today—the books we buy speak volumes (and volumes and volumes) about how we humans think. We love books that promise us a wonderful life if we follow X number of steps, tips, or checklists. Even Buddhism has plenty of lists, but the Buddha never tells us that learning the way and walking it is as easy as checking off an item on a list.

Instead, the Buddha says that teachers must *resist* the urge to try to boil things down to recipes. Trainers must not make false promises by oversimplifying the complexity of business. Learning can never be systematic, because each person learns differently. Each person must experiment, make mistakes, struggle, ask questions, explore alternatives, and find his or her own way on the path to mindful work.

The Buddha stayed with his students to help them find their paths. Nowadays, teachers can't usually do this, so they need to create a learning environment—one in which people are challenged, with problems to solve and goals to accomplish, in collaboration with others. Everything at work can be part of the awakening process.

Can the Buddha's Teachings Help Boost Employee Morale?

Get rid of your selfish mind and create a mind sincerely focused on others. Making someone happy inspires that someone to make someone else happy. In this way happiness spreads from one act.

One candle can light a myriad of others and continue to shine just as long as before. Sharing happiness never decreases it.

—Sutra of Forty-two Sections 10

I N THIS LOVELY passage the Buddha explains the basic and beautiful truth of happiness, a truth as basic to making employees happy as it is to making all living things happy.

Paradoxically, the more we work at gaining happiness, the less likely we are to experience it. Happiness doesn't come from "looking out for number one." Happiness doesn't come from "What's in it for me?"

So how do we increase employee morale and make our people happier? Look at what the Buddha did. He didn't call for more company picnics or feel-good T-shirts for everyone. Nor did he send out for pizza on Fridays. Instead, he just lived with his community; he went on alms rounds right along with the newest monk; he encouraged them with his example and with his constant presence. He shared what he had, his own happiness, and he never ran out.

The Buddha's example and presence taught even the lowliest monk that if he wanted to improve his morale, he could start where he was, by looking around for someone to share with. So if you're in that position, help someone who has something to learn or has fallen behind. Don't curse the darkness—light another's candle.

Is There Job Security in the Buddha Mind?

Being a collection of its fingers,
A hand is not an independent thing.
The same with fingers, which are made of joints.
And those joints, too, consist of smaller parts.
These parts are then divided into atoms,
And atoms split in various directions.
At last these fragments collapse into nothing.
All are empty, lacking real existence.

—Bodhicharyavatara 9.85–86

W E WOULD LIKE to have job security. We would like to have security in general. This is natural, but it's also unrealistic. In our economy, most people have long since given up the expectation of spending their whole working life with one organization. But many people still lament the passing of "the good ol' days" when employees were loyal to their organizations, and vice versa. But those good ol' days were merely a blip in the overall history of work. If you look back over the many thousands of years of human history, the notion of job security is a recent thing, occurring only in the past hundred years or less. The expectation of "job security" was a new phenomenon, brought about by the development of modern capitalism, the industrial revolution, unprecedented job choice, and the human mind's desire for permanence and stability.

In the last two decades, we have learned that job security breaks down when companies break down. The Buddha reminds us that companies always break down, like all things. We like to think of our organizations as real and solid, especially when we're counting on working there for a while. But organizations are only as solid as their structures. And structures are only as solid as their employees. And employees are only as solid as their minds and bodies. And as we have all experienced, both bodies and minds change over time.

Look what the Bodhicharyavatara is saying about our bodies. They are made up of many parts, such as feet and hands. But hands are made up of fingers, and fingers of joints, and joints of still smaller parts down to atoms and electrons and quarks and other particles that only last the briefest moment and die away. Where is the solidity in all this? The Buddha tells us it is simply nowhere. Permanence and solidity do not exist and never will.

Today we see that job security was an illusion all along—a shared myth born of desire and circumstances. We have awakened from our illusion. There is no job security and there never was. Our only job security is our ability to secure a job. Work with that.

What Might the Buddha Advise Us about Career Development Programs?

Engineers work water; fletchers arrows.
Builders master wood; the wise their selves.
—Dhammapada 80

THE WORLD IS full of rich natural resources that best meet human needs with a bit of shaping and guidance. Engineers work water into canals so that water can work for us. Fletchers make arrows for food and protection. Builders cut and carve wood into furniture and housing, to help us live more comfortable lives. All of them manage and use natural resources for our ends.

So who guides the natural resource of humanity? The Buddha says that *we* do. There is no one outside us to shape us into better humans—we must do that ourselves. Like engineers, we must channel our own energy. Like fletchers, we must sharpen our skills with precision. Like carpenters, we must smooth our minds to enjoy peace and comfort. We have the raw material of our lives with which to work, and we are responsible for what we create from that material.

This means we are also responsible for our own development as employees. We should not look for someone else to hone our skills and develop our raw talent for us. We each must do that for ourselves. A fool sits and waits, saying, "Here I am, boss. Teach me something and make of me what you will." The wise person takes the initiative and says, "Here are my career goals, these are my talents and abilities, and this is the kind of training I think I need to accomplish my goals. Can I count on your support?" The wise master themselves.

How Would a Buddha Create and Use Effective Incentives and Bonuses?

*Although gold dust is precious, when it
gets in your eye, it just causes trouble.*
— Bo Juyi, memorial inscription
for Xingshan Weikuan

SOME PEOPLE (including some Buddhists) see the Buddha as the keenest psychologist who ever lived. He understood the totality of human nature—in all its paradoxes and complexities—better than most of the therapists, psychologists, and psychiatrists who have lived in the 2,500 years (especially the last 100) since the Buddha's time. Reading the earliest teachings of Buddhism, we are shocked by how little human nature has changed in the past two and a half millennia. It's mind-boggling . . . and mind-opening.

The Buddha understood money and mind because he spent the first nearly 30 years of his life in luxury, the next 6 years in absolute poverty, and the last 45 years as the head of an order that owned great properties, but whose members owned only their staffs, their begging bowls, their toiletries, and a couple of sets of robes. He had seen money and mind from three enormously different perspectives, and he knew how to make money work for mind, not just the opposite way around.

In modern business parlance, we say, "People do what they get rewarded for." Buddhism says the same thing, just in different language. In the quote above, the poet Bo Juyi points out how easy it is to get seduced by the lure of money and overlook the true purpose of work—which is to serve others with worthwhile products and services. Given our ability to be seduced, most people work to maximize their individual rewards—often oblivious to or in denial of the effect their actions have on others. We have only to look at businessmen like Bernie Madoff to see the distortion that money can cause—and not just in others, but in *us*: no one forced anyone to invest in Bernard L. Madoff Investment Securities LLC. People—well-meaning people—made huge sums in down markets with Madoff. Some of them suspected malfeasance, but they stayed in. It was the culture on Wall Street.

Crucially, the Madoff fiasco was not isolated. It was a particularly stark example of how incentives currently work in the global economy. Those incentives have also brought us the sub-prime mortgage meltdown, the spectacular failures of institutions like financial titan Lehman Brothers and the vast Washington Mutual Bank, the global recession beginning in 2008, and so on. These collapses occurred because the compensation and bonus systems in the financial services sector rewarded behavior that, sometimes *intentionally*, bet billions against the common good.

The Buddha might smile, but it would be a sorrowful one. We have rewarded greed over effort, easy evasions over hard truths. So greed and evasion are what we have gotten. If we want different results, the Buddha would tell us to overhaul our compensation systems and incentives to reward cooperation as well as competition, and dedication over derivatives. We must design creative rewards (and punishments) that grow from a bottom line that provides worth to the world. We are the ultimate stakeholders in every corporation in every country. Corporate incentives and disincentives must acknowledge this reality. Otherwise, we'll continue to get what we rewarded last time, because in a bad system, good people often do bad things.

❀ Solving People Problems

There Are No Answers—
Pursue Them Lovingly

How Can Your Buddha Mind Inform Your Policies and Procedures?

Where is
The list
Of things
To not
Worship?

—Lawson Fusao Inada, "The List," from
"In So Doing," in *Legends from Camp*[1]

DURING THE BUDDHA'S life, the monks in his organization, the *sangha,* developed an elaborate system of rules, responding to everyday situations. Just before the Buddha died, he told the monks they could get rid of all but the few major rules. Trouble was, they couldn't discern which ones were major and which were minor, so the book of rules has grown amazingly rigid and indeed become a sacred text. This is *not* what the Buddha wanted.

Most organizations' official policies and procedures are simply another example of our human inclination to try controlling life, to make it predictable, manageable, consistent, and fair. As if demanding order were enough to create it!

While the intention to create order is not always bad, it is impossible to implement consistently. New situations and problems always arise, and we have not yet thought of rules for them. So we make more rules. We manufacture elaborate formulas and detailed explanations to make our rules precise. We publish big, fat policy manuals, so that everyone will know what the rules are (though few will read them) and our work world will be as safe, orderly, and well organized as possible. Our policies and procedures give us an answer for every eventuality . . . well, almost. We keep adding more rules, but we never delete any of the old ones. We begin to worship our policies and procedures; they become sacred texts.

The Buddha knew that rules often hurt us. We lose track of the *spirit* of the policy, and we get bogged down in the *letter* of the policy. We become ensnared in bureaucratic minutiae, tangled up and tied down in heavy cobwebs spun by busy spiders in pin-striped suits. We become paralyzed, losing the efficiency that the rules were designed to protect.

Few organizations understand this problem better than Nordstrom, the department store chain, world renowned for its superb customer service and excellent people practices. Years ago, Nordstrom's employee policy manual had just one page and one rule:

> Rule #1: Use your good judgment in all situations.
> There will be no additional rules.

The Buddha would smile.

So what would the Buddha do about policies and procedures today? If he worked anyplace other than Nordstrom, he might take the pages of his company policy manual and use them to line the bottom of a songbird's cage. When the pages were finally all gone, he would open the cage and set the songbird free.

If the Buddha Were a Diversity Consultant, What Advice Would He Give His Clients?

It is a fact that among humanity there are many diverse mental dispositions, interests, needs and so on. Therefore, the greater the diversity of religious traditions that are available, the greater their capacity to meet the needs of different people.
—The XIV Dalai Lama, *The Heart of the Buddha's Path*[2]

DIVERSITY IS A paradoxical subject for the Buddha, since at the deepest level there *is* no real diversity. Diversity implies separation of essentially separate things, but when we get down to the (non)essence of things, there is no separation—we are all not-two.

But of course, when we look around at other people, we *perceive* diversity—diversity of skin color, body shapes, age, sexual orientation, personality, work style, values, thinking patterns, skills, talents, and so on. It looks to us as though people are very different from one another, on many different levels. Since we must live on this practical level, what should we do about diversity?

The Dalai Lama, in the quote above, gives us a tip from the Buddha, using religion as his example. We should acknowledge and appreciate our human differences, and recognize the need for "different strokes for different folks." Different religions speak to different cultures; even within a culture, different people adopt different religions. This is just fine with the Buddha. He recognizes the stupidity and inadequacy of a one-size-fits-all, conformist religion. In fact, you can follow Buddhism and another religion *at the same time*. In Asia, many Buddhists are also Confucians, or Taoists, or Bon-po worshippers, or followers of a whole tapestry of different local religions. Buddhism has always adapted to the diversity of the cultures it has spread to. It's doing that here, too, in this book, for example. Buddhism, more than any other world religion, embraces diversity.

If diversity enriches religion, so should it enrich aspects of the workplace: jobs, work space, communication, work schedules, employee benefits, incentives, work styles, preferred type of leadership, and so on. We must not insist on one-size-fits-all practices, for to do so would dishonor the diversity that makes things work.

The paradox is that at a deeper level, we are all the same. We support diversity because we know that we are fundamentally so alike. We all want a fair day's pay for our work; we want appreciation and acknowledgment of our contributions; we want respect; we want interesting, meaningful work; we want to make enough money to meet our living expenses; we want kindness and compassion from others; we want to feel good about what we do for a living; and so on.

The challenge of diversity from the Buddha's perspective is to do justice to both our differences *and* our fundamental oneness. If we treat everyone exactly the same, we dishonor human diversity and uniqueness. If we treat everyone differently, how do we maintain equity and fairness?

Let us suggest the family model, for an organization is in many ways like a family. When a family includes several children, parents know that each child needs somewhat different parenting, since each child is unique. But parents know that they also have to be fair in treating each child equitably. Parents will tell you this is not easy. In fact, it is very hard. It requires constant awareness of the developmental needs of each child, balanced against the needs of the other children, and constant vigilance to maintain time, energy, discipline, attention, and love in the right proportion in each situation. This also involves frequent negotiation with the children themselves. Everyone, both parents and children, has a part to play in maintaining equity and fairness within the family.

So it is in the workplace. Everyone, both management and rank and file, has a role to play in creating a diversity-friendly, mindful organization. This requires constant communication, frequent negotiation and renegotiation, flexibility, willingness to change, and, above all, compassion and humility. Is it easy? No. Is it worth it? The Buddha says yes.

Does Having a Buddha Mind Keep You from Stereotyping?

*All women appear in the form of women, but they
appear in the form of women without being women.*
—Vimalakirtinirdesha Sutra 7

THIS IS ANOTHER version of "You can't judge a book by its cover." The sutra explains forms as artificial constructs, delusions based on our inclination to categorize people and miss their deeper Buddha nature. As humans, we are so quick to assign labels to other people: woman, man, black, white, Asian, Hispanic, old, young, straight, gay, white collar, blue collar, pink collar, management, employee, and many more. In labeling others, we think they are separate from us, that they are "other" than us. Blinkered by our stereotypes, we totally miss the point that we are all not-two; we are all interconnected and interrelated, like the individual fingers on a hand.

If we have *any* essence, it's the Buddha nature; the path of enlightenment simply shows us how to wake up to that fact. Until we wake up, we label others as inferior because we are not yet aware of our own Buddha nature and, by extension, everyone's Buddha nature.

Bottom line: those who must stereotype others deserve compassion the least but need it the most. They are asleep, bound up in desire and attachment, driven by fear and anger, much in need of enlightenment—just like ourselves, but more so. Indeed, sexists and racists appear in their forms without being those forms. Free yourself through freeing them from themselves.

How Do Buddhas Combat Sexism in the Workplace?

*You may want something, or you may be unhappy, but if you
don't let this lead you off into thinking "It's like this because
I'm only a woman,". . . [t]hen you yourself are the Buddha.*

—Zen Teacher Bankei, Hoshinji Dharma Talks

BANKEI DOESN'T MINCE words; he says as long as a woman
doesn't feel that her gender limits her, then she's already the
Buddha. If she's the Buddha, well, we reckon she can be anything
she wants to be in the workplace. So here is the first lesson on
sexism: the Buddha in you is not sexist and does not respect sexism or any other kind of prejudice. Do not sell yourself or anyone
else short on account of gender.

Here is another lesson, a history lesson this time. The historical Buddha lived in a tremendously sexist culture, 2,500 years ago.
Being a product of that culture, he was not bias-free; he believed
that an order of nuns would shorten the authority of Buddhism.
Nevertheless, he admitted that women could become Buddhas, so
he did approve the order. We estimate that in these actions he was
about 2,450 years ahead of his time. If that leaves him 50 years
behind our time, it's still a great record. Let's all strive to be 2,450
years ahead of our time. Do you think women will be fully recog-
nized as equal 2,450 years from now? Then do what the Buddha
would do and start acting on that today.

Here is lesson number three. Bankei moved forward from the
historical Buddha's position. The best forms of the Buddhist tradition are constantly evolving, growing, bettering themselves. Just
like the woman in Bankei's sermon, they are not trapped by their
problems because they are not trapped by their self-definitions.
This is the model for all of us, no matter our gender. Do not be
fettered by your own self-limiting beliefs. Even if you're a mere
man, you're still a Buddha.

Can the Buddha's Teachings Help Prevent Sexual Harassment?

People who can't get enough fame, money, and
sex are like a child licking honey off a knife blade.
—Sutra of Forty-two Sections 22

THE BUDDHA WAS clear about the kind of trouble we get ourselves into when we pursue our appetites and desires to excess. Yes, needs for peer recognition, money, and sex are normal, but they're also insatiable. If we chase after them, we're asking for trouble. It makes no difference whether you are lusting after fame, wealth, or sex; they are all desires, and they all cut like a knife.

Experts on sexual harassment agree that sexual harassment is almost never about sex at all; it's about power and domination. A sexual aggressor in the workplace is trying to demonstrate that he (94 percent of sexual harassment is initiated by men) is the alpha male who can have his pick of the females. This is basic animal behavior. Perhaps the sex is nice, but the behavior is really about who's in charge.

So what does Buddhism teach about the lust for power and control? As with all external prizes, you may win them, but it is only a matter of time before someone bigger and stronger than you takes over and becomes the new top dog. Your lust will remain, but your fulfillment will not.

So, what do we do about sexual harassment? First, we look at ourselves and make sure our own behavior is above reproach. Right speech and right action always begin with us. Then, we work to make sure everyone in our organization knows about sexual harassment laws—both the spirit of the laws and the letter of the laws. Those laws are based on respect for all individuals and the right of people to feel safe where they work (the Buddha might refer to this as the well-being of all beings). More important than knowing the law is knowing the morality of human relationships on which the law is based.

We also need to be bold in stopping harassment of any type when we see it. The welfare of individuals is dependent on the welfare of the whole group. Everyone has a stake in maintaining a harassment-free environment, because any harassment affects all workers.

How Would the Buddha Mediate between Squabbling Coworkers?

I will not be brought down by the fighting
Of childish people in their little quarrels.
Their words arise from conflict and emotion.
Instead, I'll understand and give them love.
—Bodhicharyavatara 5.56

THE BUDDHA IS, above all, compassionate. He does not judge the squabblers as bad people but simply recognizes them as squabblers. They are where they are on their own paths. We can't get discouraged, depressed, or angered when our coworkers are quarreling, any more than we get when we see children arguing on the playground. Since it's in our nature to fight, many of us will fight. We need to strive to see that these fights are as ephemeral as playground tiffs.

The Buddha tells us to understand this fact and to act lovingly. We must listen to both sides, soothing hurt feelings with patient words, helping the coworkers find common ground, and searching for compromises they all can live with. The Buddha tells us to be peacemakers, working with compassion and understanding to help others mature. Note that this does *not* necessarily mean making them happy; it means making them mindful of the other's conflicts as well as their own.

Is There Such a Thing as Compassionate Firing for Poor Performance?

The Buddha performs acts that discipline, because he wishes to show that negative actions have consequences. . . . The monk supporting the teaching does the same. Seeing an offender or harmer of the teaching, he drives them away with censure.

—Mahaparinirvana Sutra 4

O F COURSE THE Buddha teaches us not to harm others, even animals, even insects, when we can help it. But this does not mean we need to let the termites eat our whole house. Some employees are like termites. They weaken the entire business, hurting other employees, and often customers too. The Buddha would say that they have to go. Luckily, we don't have to kill them like termites, but sometimes we do have to fire them.

When someone needs discipline, we must provide discipline, sometimes even expulsion. This may be hard for us: hard because we may be reluctant to hurt the person, or hard because we may be angry at him and want to hurt him. Here we need to go back to the fundamentals: compassion and wisdom.

The Buddha tells us to fire people, but only when their negative actions have demonstrated an undesirable impact and shown that we must withhold our teaching, our company, our benefits from them. When we fire someone, we must remember why we are doing it. We fire someone because we care about every person in the workplace and every person we serve. We harm every one of them if we allow one person to undermine what we're doing, for an organization is only as strong as its weakest employee. This is wisdom.

We actually harm problem persons when we don't deal with their poor performance or misconduct, for they will never learn to do better unless they experience the consequences of their own behavior. We cannot be passive here, though we act as gently as we can. This is compassion.

So the Buddha would fire an employee reluctantly, but confidently, because he would do it for the greater good of the organization as well as of the person being fired.

The Buddha's situation was obviously different from ours today. He had followers who joined him to learn from him—they did not come together to make a product or provide a service. We can, though, still take the Buddha's lessons on justice, compassion, and community and figure out for ourselves how the Buddha might accomplish the difficult job of firing someone. Given what we know about the Buddha, he might do something like the following:

First, he would ensure that the person had been given every opportunity to succeed in his job; that he had been given appropriate training, coaching, and support along the way; and that he had not simply been thrown into a job to sink or swim on his own.

Second, the Buddha would ensure that the person had been given an opportunity to improve his performance, once it became clear that he was not living up to expectations.

If the person was still not performing up to standards, and all fairness and patience had been extended to him, the Buddha would clearly and compassionately tell him he was being fired, and facilitate a departure that was quick and clean.

The Buddha would not lie to the fired person, or to others, about the nature of the firing. For not only could that person learn much from these consequences—others could also learn from seeing that poor performance has consequences.

Above all, the Buddha would make sure at every step of this process that his heart was free from malice or revenge. Instead, his heart would be filled with loving-kindness (albeit tough love) for the person he was firing, for his other employees, and for everyone else with a stake in his organization.

What Can You Do When Mistrust Poisons Your Workplace?

> *Gods, humans, demi-gods, spirits, angels, and all other kinds*
> *of beings are bound up in envy and selfishness. This is why . . .*
> *they live in hostility, violence, rivalry, and malevolence.*
> —Digha Nikaya 21

MISTRUST IS BORN of fear, a result of perceived separation from others. If I see you as "other," I'm likely to mistrust you. Perceiving a world of scarcity, I fear there is not enough for each person and I worry about getting my share . . . of attention, acknowledgment, rewards (bonuses and pay increases), status, power, and so on. I hold on tight to my treasures and envy others. If they do the same, an entire organization becomes hostile, even violent.

If you work in such a toxic organization, there's not much you can do to change the corporate culture. But there is *something*: you can choose not to add more toxins to it. You can choose to quietly take a stand for integrity in the form of right view, right intention, right speech, and right action. Do it in small ways first, gingerly moving forward as though you were trekking through a swamp—because you are.

Start with yourself, regardless of what others are doing. This is a perfect example of being the change you wish to see in your workplace. If this becomes unsustainable for you, do the best you can to take care of yourself, and quietly begin the task of looking for a new workplace. Some workplaces are poisoned beyond healing. The company you keep in such environments will gradually destroy the character of all but the most bodhisattva-like workers. It's okay to not let this happen to you.

🝠 Organizational Change

*Everything Changes; Nothing
Remains without Change*

How Can You Handle Reorganizations, Mergers, and Acquisitions Mindfully?

Do not chase the past.
Do not pine for the future.
What is past is gone.
What is future is not yet.
What is here, what is there,
Looking, you see clearly.
Unfooled, unshaken,
you expand the heart.
Urgently do your dharma today,
because tomorrow may be too late.
There is no bargaining with death.
If you live thus mindful,
through the light and through the dark,
the sage will say, His was a good day!
　　　　　　　　　　　　—Majjhima Nikaya 131

I F YOU'VE READ the first two sections of this book before coming to the third, we think you just might know what the Buddha would say about reorganizations, mergers, and acquisitions: they're perfect embodiments of change. They're *anicca*, impermanence in action. Nothing is solid, even if it appears to be so, even if we wish it were. New things come into existence; old things go out of existence. Things fall apart and come together in new configurations. This is as true of jobs and organizations as it is of trees, fish, clouds, atomic particles, islands, and human beings.

Pema Chödrön has a wonderful twist on the classic Buddhist parable of existence—we'll paraphrase what she says. Imagine you are walking along on solid ground and you come to a river. On the other shore of the river is a different land that you think is awakening. You discover a raft on your side of the river, a raft called Buddhism. So you get in it and head across the river, hoping to reach the far shore. But halfway across the river, your boat falls apart, and there you are in the middle of shifting currents, the water roiling all around you. Your feet are frantically trying to find solid ground, and your arms are moving as you hope to grasp something that will make you feel more secure. But your kicking and grasping will not gain any shore, only the formless current. When you make peace with that reality and relax into it, you will awaken to the only peace, the only goal there is. This is learning to be mindful; this is a good day.

Likewise, the waters are constantly moving in the turbulent Sea of Organizations. Currents swell one way; the tide surges another. The winds of change blow strong, and the waves roll and crash, sometimes on top of you. You may cling to the wreckage of the past and wish you could bring back the good old days, but there is nothing left but flotsam and jetsam.

The Buddha would understand your distress and empathize with your longing for solid ground; nonetheless, he would gently but firmly teach you to swim, surf, paddle, or just float for a while. Maybe, when you're a full bodhisattva, you'll walk on the water—for right now, the Buddha would just say, "Love it."

What Can We Do about Outsourcing?

Whenever Buddhism has taken root in a new land, there has been a certain variation in the style in which it is observed. The Buddha himself taught differently according to the place, the occasion and the situation of those who were listening to him.
—The XIV Dalai Lama, Letter to the Fourth
International Conference of Buddhist Women

THE BUDDHA'S TEACHINGS show us again and again how we are all interconnected and interdependent. Separateness is an illusion. Recall the metaphor of the hand from the answer on job security. You may think that you have four separate fingers and a thumb. But if you look a little closer and think a little longer, you realize that your fingers and thumb are all connected together at the palm of your hand. And not only are they physically connected by flesh, blood, bone, and nerves; they work together in a coordinated fashion to get things done. Your hand is a wonderful model of interconnection, interdependence, and cooperative coordination; as Thich Nhat Hanh would say, it *inter-is*.

So, too, inter-are the worlds of business, commerce, government, philanthropy, medicine, agriculture, banking, and higher education. Our world, and all the countries in it, is interconnected in ways that most of us can't see or fathom. Currency fluctuations in Europe affect the cost of goods sold in the United States. Changes in the education and skill levels of workers in one part of the world affect where multinational corporations do their work. Money ebbs and flows; people and jobs move; power and influence shift—all is impermanent.

To the extent that we can adapt to shifting job markets and literally go with the flow, we will know peace. If we rail against change and lament the injustice of jobs moving here and there around the planet, we will suffer. There are no other choices, and the choice is ours.

We can be the thumb who complains that our job was outsourced to the fingers, or we can be flexible and develop new skills to fit ourselves with new work. The Buddha would suggest that we join with the fingers in cooperation—typing on a keyboard, carrying boxes, using tools, or folding our hands in prayer and gratitude.

How Can Buddhist Principles Help in Dealing with a Corporate Crisis or Scandal?

Through attention, effort, and restraint,
The wise make islands floods cannot erode.

—Dhammapada 25

RECENT BUSINESS HISTORY and today's news pages confirm the wisdom of the Buddha's words. Remember how well Johnson & Johnson came through the Tylenol tampering crisis, back in 1982? The CEO took initiative instantly, pulling Tylenol products from store shelves, at enormous cost to the company. The speed and wisdom of his response to a deadly crisis ensured that the company would rebound, which it did with renewed public confidence and resulting strong sales. This is how to handle a crisis effectively. But this example is 30 years old.

Unfortunately, we see far too many examples of how *not* to handle a crisis. Calculating damage control and manipulating the audience is not the way. Consider these crises: the phone hacking by News Corp. employees, the nuclear accident at Chernobyl, Hurricane Katrina, a sexual scandal in the highest office in America, endemic child abuse in the Catholic Church. When these crises hit, spin did not help. Wisdom was called for but was not forthcoming. The damage was permanent.

Crises happen to all kinds of organizations: military, government, health care, church, philanthropic, professional, and so on. You cannot protect your organization from all crises, but you *can* help ensure that you and your organization are not destroyed by them. Think of the Buddha as the first crisis management consultant and heed his advice: through attention, effort, and restraint, you stand firm as the crisis swirls. You are ready to work again when the flood subsides.

How Does a Buddha Turn around a Troubled Business?

My supernatural power and marvelous activity:
drawing water and chopping wood.

—The Record of Layman Pang

IN INDIA, HOLY persons are expected to perform miracles—Buddhas included. But the Buddha taught his followers not to reveal any miraculous powers in public. Why is this? Because such powers distract people from what really matters. People get all absorbed in the supernatural, and they forget to attend to the natural, the things that form the backbone of life—and work. Layman Pang shows us how Buddhism and work are all about being there and getting it done without complications and without show.

Why do organizations fail? The reasons are varied, of course, but often it's because they lose sight of the fundamentals. They don't get done what they need to get done. If you're making a product, you have to make it well and price it right. This is not so complicated. It's about focusing your attention on the basics, just like Layman Pang, living in his forest hut, getting water and wood: simple and essential. The core activities of an organization are what keeps everything going and makes the organization successful. In today's language, we would say, pay attention to "where the rubber meets the road." It's the modern equivalent of "drawing water and chopping wood."

The Buddha would turn around a floundering business by getting back to basics, making sure there was water and wood when needed. Even at the top of an enormous corporation, the boss has got to remember this. Think, for example, of Apple Computer. It was floundering in the late '90s and given up for dead by many business analysts. The company brought back its visionary founder, Steve Jobs, to turn it around. What marvelous thing did he do first? He slashed the product line and the budget to focus on designs that worked. He got back to Apple's basic strength. Does that reveal miraculous powers? No, but it sure was miraculous for the stock price.

It is basics, always the basics, that make things run. Not necessarily core products, but core processes. Sure, there must be vision, but vision doesn't create anything without good ol' simple work. Drawing water, chopping wood.

How Does a Buddha Start a New Business?

Now mountains are mind; rivers are mind; earth, sun, moon, and stars are mind. In this moment, what appears before you?
—Dogen Zenji, Shinjin Gakudo

IF YOU LOOK around you, no matter where you are, virtually everything you see—except natural objects (if you're Dogen, *even* natural objects)—began as an idea in someone's mind. Skyscrapers, telephone poles, roads, carpets, smart phones, TVs, bedpans, cardigans, microwaves, and Mini Coopers—each material thing in the human world began in a human mind.

So that is where the Buddha would go for inspiration: mind is the source. Look at the first words of the Dhammapada: "All things come at first from mind. / Mind creates them, mind fulfills them." The Buddha would trust his imagination and intuition over trends and tweets. He'd follow his muse.

Next, he would talk to people about their lifestyles, their interests, their needs. The Buddha knew that happiness and success come from serving others, so he would look for ways to put his unique talents and skills in service. He would look at demographic shifts and changes in people's lifestyles, here and abroad (remember, we inter-are). New needs grow from these changes, and new needs mean new openings for business. His guiding questions would be, "What do people need and want now?" and "How can I fill those needs?"

The Buddha would think about money, of course, but that would not be his primary incentive or concern. The Buddha knew that financial success comes as a happy by-product of providing needed products and services. Money is simply a way of keeping score—telling you whether or not goods and services are meeting people's needs and desires. Meet needs, and you never need to think about making money.

The Buddha would surround himself with people who shared his values. He would hire kind people who understood teamwork. The Buddha knows that you can give workers a new skill, but you cannot give them a new character. He would model interbeing. He would show his workers how they could be more successful in collaborating rather than competing with one another. He'd understand their needs and be happy for them to telecommute, take advantage of flextime, and so on.

The Buddha's new business would be green. He understood sustainability, that humans are interdependent not only with other humans but with all living beings—indeed, all inanimate things as well. The Buddha's business would be a good steward of environmental resources, recognizing that stewardship is the highest form of leadership.

And finally, the Buddha would be humble. No need to plaster his name on tall buildings. Since he would wear modest clothes and live in a modest house, he wouldn't need a seven-figure salary. He'd use the same bathroom as his employees and eat with them in the cafeteria. He would carpool.

The Buddha would reinvest his profits in innovation, always taking risks. When his business was flush, he would give plenty of money away to reduce *dukkha* at its sources. And he'd remember that someday his business would pass away, as all things must. Everything is impermanent, even a Buddha's business.

anicca   Impermanence. See *three marks*, below.

anatta   Literally, "no self" or "no soul." See *three marks*, below.

bodhisattva   Literally, "awakening being"; a person who works to achieve liberation with and for all living beings. The highest goal of Mahayana Buddhism is to be a bodhisattva.

bodhisattva path   In Mahayana Buddhism, the practice of devoting oneself to the awakening of all beings. The path extends over lifetimes; indeed, since living beings are innumerable, this selfless path is endless.

Buddha   Literally, "awakened one," an awakened being; the first of the three jewels of Buddhism; one who reveals the teachings of Buddhism to the world. According to Buddhism, Gautama Siddhartha (a.k.a. Shakyamuni Buddha) was the Buddha for our historical era, but there are many others for other times and places.

Buddhadharma   The teaching of the Buddha (see *dharma*).

Buddha nature / Buddha mind   The inherent potential in all beings to become or act as Buddhas. A core teaching of Mahayana Buddhism holds that we are all potentially Buddhas already, because we have this mind. Thus, awakening is not an achievement but a liberation of our own true nature.

compassion   Sympathy and love for all beings; one of the two principal Buddhist virtues (the other is wisdom). Compassion is said to give rise to the wish to free all beings from dukkha. This, in turn, motivates us to become bodhisattvas, or at least to act toward others with kindness and understanding.

dharma or dhamma   Sanskrit and Pali words meaning several things. In Buddhist contexts they usually mean the truth, the word of the Buddha, the Buddha's teachings. Dharma is the second of the three jewels of Buddhism.

dukkha   Literally, "dissatisfaction" or "dis-ease"; the existential suffering caused by desires and attachments. We all have dukkha as long as we cling to our selves. See *three marks*, below.

eightfold noble path   The basic Buddhist way of living. An expansion of the "middle path." This way of living is divided into eight factors organized into three groups. Right speech, right action, and right livelihood form the ethical part of practice. Right effort, right mindfulness, and right meditation are the second group, concerned with training the mind. Right view and right intention form the wisdom aspect of understanding. When we fully embody all the path factors, we are Buddhas.

four noble truths   The Buddha's first teachings after his awakening: (1) we all have suffering and dissatisfaction; (2) this suffering and dissatisfaction is caused by ignorance, desire, and attachment; (3) this suffering and dissatisfaction can end; (4) suffering and dissatisfaction are ended through following the eightfold path.

haiku   A Japanese poetic form strongly associated with Zen Buddhism. Haiku in Japanese are composed of three lines of five, seven, and five syllables. In English the syllable count may vary.

karma   The effects of our acting with our body, speech, and mind. These actions and their effects serve as the cause for future events, even rebirths. Skillful actions cause positive results. *Karma* is often used in the popular sense as "What goes around comes around" or "As you sow, so shall you reap."

lama   An incarnation of a Vajrayana spiritual teacher or guru; the highest is the Dalai Lama. Other forms of Buddhism do not have lamas, but Vajrayana holds that highly advanced teachers may choose their rebirths and that their followers may identify those reborn teachers at a very young age and train them.

Mahayana Literally, "greater vehicle"; the form of Buddhism predominant in East Asia. Mahayana emphasizes the bodhisattva path.

metta Loving-kindness, the feeling we naturally radiate when we break through the delusion of our separate selves. Buddhists work to cultivate this feeling for all beings.

middle path / middle way Synonyms for "Buddhism." The Buddha taught the middle path between self-indulgence and self-denial in his very first sermon.

nirvana Liberation from *samsara* (rebirth in the universe). Usually defined as freedom from the illusions of the self that cause dukkha.

paticca-samuppada Dependent co-arising, the condition of everything coming into being due to other factors and other things. Since everything is like this, we are all interconnected in profound ways. The Vietnamese teacher Thich Nhat Hanh translates this word as "interbeing." For him, we all inter-are.

Pure Land The Buddha land of Amida Buddha, in which enlightenment is easy to experience; tens of millions of Mahayana Buddhists pray to be reborn there, many believing that the Pure Land is within ourselves and our rebirth there can take place *now*.

right livelihood One of the eight factors of the eightfold noble path; work that does little or no harm to all living things. We also might define it as what we all need to strive to make our own jobs become.

roshi Literally, "old man"; the title for senior Japanese Zen teachers.

samsara This universe of repeated existence; the world where we must continuously be reborn, die, be reborn, die . . .

sangha Literally, "group." Generally, the Buddhist community, our spiritual friends. Sometimes sangha is used to mean monastics only, sometimes to mean all followers on the path. Sangha is the third of the three jewels of Buddhism.

Shakyamuni Buddha Literally, "The Sage of the Shakyas"; Gautama Siddhartha of the Shakya clan, the historical Buddha.

shunya Literally, "hollow" or "open." See *shunyata*.

shunyata Openness (often badly translated as "emptiness"); the belief that all things are empty of inherent existence—that they do not exist except in an endless web of relations. A Mahayana development of the core Buddhist teachings of impermanence and lack of self.

sutra or sutta Sanksrit and Pali words, respectively, meaning a teaching of the Buddha. Traditionally, these sutras are considered the actual words of the Buddha. Collections of these sutras, with the monastic rules and the early commentaries, form the canons, the sacred scriptures of the various forms of Buddhism.

tao (pronounced "dow") Literally, "the way"; a central concept of East Asian religion, including Buddhism. Taoists are those practicing Taoism, the religion flowing from the power, balance, and ease of following the natural way of things. Taoism, Buddhism, and Confucianism formed the "three traditions," the religious complex of traditional Chinese culture.

Theravada Literally, "the way of the elders"; the form of Buddhism predominant in South and Southeast Asia. Theravada focuses on the community of monastics striving for awakening.

three jewels The Buddha, the dharma, and the sangha: traditionally, what a person needs to rely on, or take refuge in, to reach awakening.

three marks   The three basic qualities of life: dukkha, anicca, anatta (suffering, impermanence, no-self). The first is the result of not understanding the second. The third is a special case of the second that is exceptionally hard for us to accept. Buddhist wisdom sees into the heart of all three.

three poisons   Greed, hatred, and delusion, the roots of our human troubles. Through practice we try to negate these, eventually transforming them into their opposites: generosity, loving-kindness, and wisdom.

upaya   Usually translated as "skillful means"; it can be any kind of speech or action that leads toward awakening, but usually refers to actions done for another person, especially when those actions might otherwise seem unrelated to Buddhism or even misleading.

wisdom   An understanding of things that goes beyond intellectual knowing; one of the two principal Buddhist virtues (the other is compassion). Wisdom comes from seeing the world and ourselves as we really are (and aren't), and gives us freedom from egocentric suffering.

Zen Buddhism   Literally, "meditation Buddhism"; the East Asian Buddhist tradition emphasizing the struggle to realize one's original nature. In English, we usually say "Zen," the Japanese name, but the tradition is called Chan in China, Son in Korea, and Tien in Vietnam.

A Word about Sources

Traditionally, the words in the suttas assembled in the five *nikayas* ("groups" or "collections") are accepted as the *ipsissima verba*, the actual words of the Buddha. So, when we quote from any text that has the word *Nikaya* in its title, we are quoting the Buddha directly.

We also quote from many other sutras and texts not in those collections. Two of these sources, the Bodhicharyavatara and the Dhammapada, deserve special mention here.

The Bodhicharyavatara is a book-length poem written by the monk Shantideva over a thousand years ago. Unusually for a Buddhist text, it attends closely to the needs and troubles of us householders. That is, we folks who work instead of meditate for a living. For this reason, we quote the Bodhicharyavatara often and recommend it highly.

The Dhammapada is an early compendium of many short phrases and teachings of the Buddha. It is both powerful and pithy—a rare combination. The Dhammapada is one of the most beloved texts in the Buddhist tradition, and one of our favorites, as you can see in this book.

Notes

Part I: Becoming a Mindful Worker

Choosing Mindful Work: Creating Right Livelihood

1. Steven Sanfield, "A Poem for Those of You Who Are Sometimes Troubled by Barking Dogs and Low Flying Jets," in *American Zen: By a Guy Who Tried It* (Monterey, KY: Larkspur Press, 1994), 29.

Practical Enlightenment: Chop Wood, Carry Water

1. Shunyu Suzuki, *Zen Mind, Beginner's Mind* (New York and Tokyo: Weatherhill, 1970), 21.

Quality of Work Life: The Middle Way at Work

1. Philip Toshio Sudo, *Zen Computer: Mindfulness and the Machine* (New York: Simon & Schuster, 1999), 67.
2. Robert Aitken, *Encouraging Words: Zen Buddhist Teachings for Western Students* (New York: Pantheon, 1993), 116.

Being Successful: How Do You Define Success?

1. Bstan-'dzin-rgya-mtsho (the XIV Dalai Lama), *The Spirit of Tibet, Vision for Human Liberation: Selected Speeches and Writings of HH the Dalai Lama* (New Delhi: Tibetan Parliamentary and Policy Research Centre in association with Vikas Publishing House, 1996), 253.

Money and Happiness: What's the Connection?

1. Bhante Henepola Gunaratana, rev. ed., *Mindfulness in Plain English* (Boston: Wisdom Publications, 1996), 41.

Dealing with Change: Riding the Waves of Impermanence

1. Ajahn Brahm, *Who Ordered This Truckload of Dung?: Inspiring Stories for Welcoming Life's Difficulties* (Boston: Wisdom Publications, 2005), 257–58.
2. Pema Chödrön, *The Places That Scare You: A Guide to Fearlessness in Difficult Times* (Boston: Shambhala Publications, 2002), 18.
3. Anne Cushman, "What Is Death, Mommy?" in *The Best Buddhist Writing 2006* (Boston: Shambhala Publications, 2006), 59.
4. Lama Thubten Yeshe, *The Bliss of Inner Fire: Heart Practice of the Six Yogas of Naropa* (Boston: Wisdom Publications, 1998), 41.
5. Pema Chödrön, *Start Where You Are: A Guide to Compassionate Living* (Boston: Shambhala Publications, 2004), 6.

Part II: Cultivating Mindful Work Relationships

Working with Others: Unity in Diversity

1. David Chadwick, *To Shine One Corner of the World: Moments with Shunryu Suzuki* (New York: Broadway Books, 2001), 245.
2. Thich Nhat Hanh, *Peace Is Every Step: The Path of Mindfulness in Everyday Life* (New York: Bantam Books, 1991), 91.

Customers—Love 'Em or Lose 'Em: Customer Service as Bodhisattva Activity

1. The XIV Dalai Lama, in *The Dalai Lama: A Policy of Kindness* (Ithaca, NY: Snow Lion Publications, 1990), 51.

Part III: Creating a Mindful Workplace

1. Dona Witten and Akong Tulku Rinpoche, *Enlightened Management: Bringing Buddhist Principles to Work* (Rochester, VT: Park Street Press, 1999), 3.

The Big Issues: Beyond the Bottom Line

1. Christina Feldman and Jack Kornfield, eds, *Stories of the Spirit, Stories of the Heart: Parables of the Spiritual Path from Around the World* (San Francisco: HarperCollins, 1991), 250.

Work Practices and Processes: Practice Is Awakening

1. Philip Toshio Sudo, *Zen Computer: Mindfulness and the Machine* (New York: Simon & Schuster, 1999), 40–41.

The Care and Feeding of Employees: Your Team as Your Sangha

1. Ani Tenzin Palmo, *Reflections on a Mountain Lake: Teachings on Practical Buddhism* (Ithaca, NY: Snow Lion Publications), 132–33.

Solving People Problems: There Are No Answers—Pursue Them Lovingly

1. Lawson Fusao Inada, "The List," from "In So Doing" in *Legends from Camp* (Minneapolis: Coffee House Press, 1993), 140.
2. The XIV Dalai Lama, *The Heart of the Buddha's Path* (London: Thorson's, 2000), 71.

Franz Metcalf Franz's background and varied professional achievements combine the spiritual and the scholarly, religious feeling and critical thinking. He began his graduate studies of religion 25 years ago, getting his master's degree at the Graduate Theological Union, comparing Buddhist and Catholic spiritual practices. He earned a doctoral fellowship at the University of Chicago and pursued his abiding personal interest in Zen by writing his dissertation on the question, "Why do Americans practice Zen Buddhism?" He was awarded distinction on both his doctoral exams and his dissertation, receiving his PhD in 1997.

In the ivory tower, Franz is president of the American Academy of Religion, Western Region, and has participated in numerous scholarly meetings, in addition to organizing one—which is harder. He has published various articles and chapters on contemporary Buddhism and is book review editor of the *Journal of Global Buddhism* (http:// www.globalbuddhism.org). Franz teaches religious studies at California State University, Los Angeles.

Down from the tower, Franz is a founding member of the Forge Institute for Spirituality and Social Change. He is also author of four other books, including *What Would Buddha Do?*, a best seller published in a dozen languages. He continues to inquire into Buddhism and psychology, both academically and personally. And he says hi to his daughter Pearl. He's also working on a historical-spiritual detective novel. Prayers might be in order.

You can reach Franz at franz@mind2mind.net. For seminars, keynote speeches, workshops, and kvetching, you can reach both Franz and BJ at their Web site http://www.buddhaatwork.com.

BJ Gallagher BJ sees her work as a spiritual calling. She preaches the gospel of compassionate management and wise people practices, helping her clients create a kinder, gentler workplace.

BJ has built her business on the success of her international best seller, *A Peacock in the Land of Penguins* (23 languages; over 350,000 copies), as well as her other business books, *YES Lives in the Land of NO* and *It's Never Too Late to Be What You Might Have Been*. She also develops assessment tools and produces training videos.

Among BJ's clients are corporations, professional associations, nonprofit groups, and government agencies, including IBM, Chevron, Kellogg, Toyota, Chrysler, Volkswagen, American Press Institute, and the U.S. Department of Veterans Affairs. She has conducted seminars and delivered keynotes in Latin America, Canada, and Europe.

BJ is a Phi Beta Kappa graduate of the University of Southern California, where she also pursued (but never caught) a PhD in social ethics. She wrote her first book, *Telling Your Story, Exploring Your Faith*, while she was the director of staff development at USC. She then moved on to serve as training manager for the *Los Angeles Times*.

In writing *Being Buddha at Work*, BJ has come full circle, integrating her interest in spirituality with her business expertise.

You can reach BJ at bbjjgallagher@aol.com. For illuminating seminars, inspiring keynote speeches, and engaging workshops, you can reach both Franz and BJ at their Web site, http://www.buddhaat work.com.

Berrett–Koehler
Publishers

Berrett-Koehler is an independent publisher dedicated to an ambitious mission: *Creating a World That Works for All*.

We believe that to truly create a better world, action is needed at all levels—individual, organizational, and societal. At the individual level, our publications help people align their lives with their values and with their aspirations for a better world. At the organizational level, our publications promote progressive leadership and management practices, socially responsible approaches to business, and humane and effective organizations. At the societal level, our publications advance social and economic justice, shared prosperity, sustainability, and new solutions to national and global issues.

A major theme of our publications is "Opening Up New Space." Berrett-Koehler titles challenge conventional thinking, introduce new ideas, and foster positive change. Their common quest is changing the underlying beliefs, mindsets, institutions, and structures that keep generating the same cycles of problems, no matter who our leaders are or what improvement programs we adopt.

We strive to practice what we preach—to operate our publishing company in line with the ideas in our books. At the core of our approach is stewardship, which we define as a deep sense of responsibility to administer the company for the benefit of all of our "stakeholder" groups: authors, customers, employees, investors, service providers, and the communities and environment around us.

We are grateful to the thousands of readers, authors, and other friends of the company who consider themselves to be part of the "BK Community." We hope that you, too, will join us in our mission.

A BK Life Book

This book is part of our BK Life series. BK Life books change people's lives. They help individuals improve their lives in ways that are beneficial for the families, organizations, communities, nations, and world in which they live and work. To find out more, visit **www.bk-life.com**.

Berrett–Koehler
Publishers

A community dedicated to creating
a world that works for all

Visit Our Website: www.bkconnection.com

Read book excerpts, see author videos and Internet movies, read
our authors' blogs, join discussion groups, download book apps, find
out about the BK Affiliate Network, browse subject-area libraries of
books, get special discounts, and more!

Subscribe to Our Free E-Newsletter, the *BK Communiqué*

Be the first to hear about new publications, special discount offers,
exclusive articles, news about bestsellers, and more! Get on the list
for our free e-newsletter by going to **www.bkconnection.com**.

Get Quantity Discounts

Berrett-Koehler books are available at quantity discounts for orders
of ten or more copies. Please call us toll-free at (800) 929-2929 or
email us at bkp.orders@aidcvt.com.

Join the BK Community

BKcommunity.com is a virtual meeting place where people from
around the world can engage with kindred spirits to create a world
that works for all. BKcommunity.com members may create their own
profiles, blog, start and participate in forums and discussion groups,
post photos and videos, answer surveys, announce and register for
upcoming events, and chat with others online in real time. Please join
the conversation!

MIX
From responsible
sources
FSC® C004691

Certified

Corporation
bcorporation.net